MARTIN WOOD

SISTER PARISH

AMERICAN STYLE

FRANCES LINCOLN LIMITED
PUBLISHERS

MARTIN WOOD

SISTER PARISH

AMERICAN STYLE

F

FRANCES LINCOLN LIMITED
PUBLISHERS

For one who had a verdant heart

Frances Lincoln Limited
4 Torriano Mews
Torriano Avenue
London NW5 2RZ
www.franceslincoln.com

Sister Parish
American Style
Copyright © Frances Lincoln 2011
Text copyright © Martin Wood 2011
For copyright in the illustrations see page 208.

A catalogue record for this book is available from the British Library.

ISBN 978-0-7112-3219-8

Designed by Caroline Clark

Printed and bound in China

9 8 7 6 5 4 3 2 1

PAGES 2–3 AND ENDPAPERS Parish-Hadley 'Waldingfeld' in green
PAGES 4–5 Parish-Hadley 'Desmond' in pale sage and gold

CONTENTS

WHERE IT ALL BEGAN

May Tuckerman Kinnicutt and Gustav Hermann Kinnicutt, Sister's parents, sitting on the garden steps at Mayfields, their home in Far Hills, New Jersey. **PREVIOUS PAGES** Parish-Hadley 'Clara B' in yellow.

WHERE IT ALL BEGAN

Although her nickname might suggest someone of a religious disposition, dedicated to a life of prayer and penitence, the good works to which Dorothy May 'Sister' Parish devoted her life were of quite a different nature. The *grand dame* of twentieth-century American decorators, 'Sister' (as she was known from childhood) is widely credited with developing the 'American Style' of decoration, a look as distinctive as the 'English Country House Style' favoured by Nancy Lancaster and John Fowler across the Atlantic in England.

Like Nancy Lancaster, Sister Parish was born in the United States. But while Nancy was intensely proud of her Virginian roots, Dorothy Parish was a Yankee, a northerner through and through, and equally proud of that. She was born on 15 July 1910 at Morristown, New Jersey.[1] Her parents were wealthy, but not vastly rich. Her paternal grandfather, Dr Francis Kinnicutt, was an eminent physician and head of the Presbyterian Hospital in New York.[2] He married Eleanora Kissel, the daughter of a German banking family who had settled in New York. Their son Gustav Hermann Kinnicutt (1877–1943), Sister's father, was a New York stockbroker who formed, with his uncle Gustav Kissel, the brokerage firm of Kissel–Kinnicutt.[3]

Sister can never have known her grandmother Kinnicutt, for she died in October 1910, when Sister was a few months old. However, this did not stop her later describing Eleanora as 'a woman of distinct character and frozen expression – all bust, bustles, and severity'.[4] She seems to have devoted considerable energy to placing 'No Spitting' signs all round the New York subway (a rather futile occupation). The Kinnicutts seem to have had no taste – that mysterious quality without which it is impossible to create a beautiful home. For, as Sister was to recall, her grandparents' houses in New York and Morristown were 'large, dark and musty', full of 'polar bear rugs, moose heads, and antlers everywhere, golden oak furniture and dreary pastoral paintings'.[5]

Her mother's side of the family was a completely different matter. Sister's mother, May Appleton Tuckerman (1887–1947), came from an old Yankee family. Among her ancestors were the Puritan minister Cotton Mather, who played an important part in the Salem witch trials, and Oliver Wolcott, who was one of the signatories of the Declaration of Independence. Wolcott's son, Oliver Junior, was secretary to the treasury in the administrations of George Washington and John Adams. His daughter Laura married Colonel George Gibbs, a wealthy gentleman of Newport, Rhode Island, and their daughter Elizabeth married Lucius Tuckerman in 1844. Lucius Tuckerman (Sister's great-grandfather) became a pioneer in the manufacture of iron, developing with his brother Joseph a form of iron known as 'Ulster iron', with extremely high tensile strength. He lived in New York at Washington Place and then Madison Avenue, before moving to Washington, D.C., where he built a large house on the corner of 16th and First streets. The house, long since demolished, had a fine collection of paintings, as did his country home at Stockbridge, Massachusetts, where he died in 1890.

Lucius's son Bayard was Sister's grandfather. Bayard lectured on English literature for almost ten years at Princeton University, but his wife, Annie Appleton Tuckerman, disliked Princeton, and eventually he gave up his position.[6] They spent the rest of their lives in New York, at 118 East 37th Street, and at Ipswich, Massachusetts, where they had a house called Sunswick, built on part of the family estate which had been owned by Appletons, Annie Tuckerman's family, for three centuries. Annie Tuckerman, according to Sister, was 'a pretty, frail woman of enormous charm'. She also, by all accounts, had a sharp and ready wit – which was inherited by Sister.[7] The Tuckermans, unlike the Kinnicutts, were noted for their good taste; and they produced not only Sister Parish but also another renowned decorator, Dorothy Draper, who was a cousin.[8]

Gustav Kinnicutt and May Tuckerman were married in 1907, in New York, at the Church of the Incarnation on Madison Avenue and 35th Street. The wedding was one of the largest and grandest of the 1907 season. The names on the guest list read like a who's who of New York society: among them featured Joseph Choate, former ambassador to the Court of St James; Mrs Grover Cleveland (her husband was 22nd and 24th President of the United States); Mrs J. Pierpont Morgan, wife of the famous financier; the Payne Whitneys; and members of the Winthrop family.[9] After the ceremony they all retired to the 'old Dodge mansion' (on Fifth Avenue and 61st Street), loaned for the occasion, where the reception was held.

They settled at East 36th Street in the Murray Hill area of New York and at a cottage in Morristown, New Jersey – probably on Sussex Avenue where there were many Kinnicutt and Kissel properties. The Kinnicutts' first child, Francis Parker, 'Frankie', was born in 1908, with Dorothy May coming two years later. Gustav Hermann, 'Gory', followed in 1912 and Bayard, 'Birdie', in 1918.[10] Dorothy seems to have been known as 'Dot' for a little while, but Frankie soon

Frankie, Birdie, Gory and Sister in the garden at Mayfields.

Gustav Kinnicutt with Frankie and Sister.

christened her 'Sister' and, as she was indeed the only sister of three brothers, it is perhaps not surprising that this was the nickname that stuck. From photographs it is apparent that Sister had inherited the good looks of her family, their dark hair, piercing eyes and charming smile. However, according to Sister herself, 'I was a hideous baby. After staring for days at my scrunched-up face and straight brown hair, my father finally pried my eyes open only to discover that they were dull brown. "We'll always dress her in brown," Mother is reported to have said. "It's our only possible hope."' Even her aunt Joan Tuckerman, who was 'hopelessly sentimental about every member of our family, admitted that I was a hideous baby.'[11] Sister seems to have been closest to her middle brother, 'Gory'. The boys were all packed off to St Mark's School, Southborough, Massachusetts, while Sister was sent to Peck School in Morristown, New Jersey, in the spring and autumn and to Miss Chapin's School in New York during the winter. Perhaps this split education was not such a good idea, for it is said that when asked what she had learnt after finishing first grade she replied that 'George Washington is Jesus' father'. Her parents did their best to equip her with all the usual accomplishments of a girl of her class, including ballet, sewing and even fencing, but apparently to no avail. A large piano was purchased and a teacher engaged to teach her to play, but this proved peculiarly painful to the ear, and the attempt was soon abandoned.

Miss Chapin's School, mindful that they needed to show that a pupil was making some progress to justify their fees, suggested that Sister should be taken for examination by a doctor. An appointment was made with a psychiatrist, Dr Draper, who was a distant relative. When he asked, 'Do you like school?', her mother replied 'No'. When she was asked, 'Do you like riding?', her mother replied 'Yes', and when she was asked, 'Do you believe in God?', her mother answered 'No'. Dr Draper understood the problem and advised that the mother stay to be analysed.

Though 'I never learned a thing at school and never tried to', Sister did manage to make it through eighth grade, after which she was sent to Foxcroft School in Middleburg, Virginia. Founded in 1914 by Charlotte Noland (a relative of Nancy Lancaster's), it had rapidly become *the* finishing school for girls from wealthy East Coast families. The regime was not for the faint-hearted. However, Sister developed a cunning way to spend more time in the infirmary, which she found decidedly more comfortable than the classroom. She discovered that by pressing a tender spot on the bridge of her nose she would get a nosebleed. Somehow – quite how even she was at a loss to explain – she won a prize for punctuality and was runner-up for the good manners prize.

Her parents had also spent considerable sums on travel to Europe, in the hope that exposure to great art and architecture would improve their children's education. They travelled in some style, staying at grand hotels, and on one occasion touring in a Hispano-Suiza motor car. Sister maintained that throughout all the traipsing around palaces, museums and cathedrals she had resolutely kept her eyes closed and succeeded in learning absolutely nothing. Given the style and nature of her subsequent work, this seems unlikely.

A significant event of Sister's childhood was the building of the Parish house in New Jersey. Gustav Kinnicutt's business had flourished during the First World War and this enabled him to buy the 250-acre estate of Knollcrest in Far Hills, New Jersey, in 1919. Knollcrest had been built in the mid-1890s by John Forrest Dillon. It was a great barn of a place, shingle-hung and bedecked by gables, turrets and dormers. Recognizing the impossibility of adapting the house, Gustav Kinnicutt wisely had it torn down.[12] He engaged the New York architects Cross & Cross to design a new house, to be christened Mayfields after his wife. The two brothers John Walter Cross – who actually designed Mayfields – and Eliot B. Cross had an important New York architectural practice

Totcroft.   1915.

and were well connected socially. They designed the Tiffany building on Fifth Avenue and 57th Street in New York, and the Art Deco RCA building on Lexington Avenue, as well as many mansions in the Somerset Hills around Far Hills.

Gustav Kinnicutt must have been an exacting client, for he pored over every plan, examining every detail, considering at length how the sun would fall in each room throughout the day and over the year. This attention paid off. Built to an informal meandering design of fieldstone and brick, with a service wing of stuccoed block, all nestling under a grey slate roof, the house, though substantial in size, appears modest and charming. The first article published about it, in *House Beautiful* in 1923, was entitled 'A large house that looks small'. And so it is.

Sister had some clear recollections of their previous home in Morristown. When she was six years old her parents redecorated much of the house, including the sitting room, which she loved and long remembered: 'The walls were white, the floors covered with pale yellow matting and a needlework rug of strewn white roses, tattered and worn. The furniture was wicker, painted white, upright and stiff.'[13] She was to be very fond of white-painted furniture all her life.

What is also interesting is her recall of small details. She continued: 'The backs and seats of the chairs had hard cushions, padded and buttoned. I remember the buttons would pop off, leaving little strings. I felt sorry for those buttons and tried to put them back on. The material of the cushions and curtains was a heavy white cotton printed with vines and roses.' The room was later redone – probably by the New York decorators Schmidt Brothers – the wicker was 'replaced with American antiques, overstuffed sofas and chairs appeared, and new ornaments infiltrated the room – wax flowers, Staffordshire animals, loving china couples,

The garden façade of Mayfields.

tufted flower pictures, and oil paintings of valleys and streams.'[14] But the memory of the earlier room was to linger with her.

At about the same time as they began building Mayfields the Kinnicutts gave up their New York house at East 36th Street and moved to a far larger house, 65 East 82nd Street. Arranged over six floors, the house even had its own elevator. Gustav Kinnicutt was a connoisseur of English and American furniture and the house reflected this. Schmidts found a pine-panelled library in England, which was bought, shipped and reassembled. In a great white and gold panelled drawing room – an echo of high Edwardian taste – acres of old parquet floors were elegantly reflected in Queen Anne looking glasses. 'English, all English', was how Gustav liked to describe the house, but there was one exception: Sister's bedroom, which had canopied beds and a highboy, all of which was distinctly early American.[15]

Mayfields was also 'English, all English', or rather it was an American interpretation of English style. It sat at the end of a long winding drive and even today looks very much as it did when it was built, the only changes to the façade being subtle (most notably, a porch arrangement has been removed to leave the elegant pedimented door case). In the elegant parquet-floored entrance hall the most beautiful – and decidedly American – feature was a sweeping staircase, which has been restored or rather reinstated by the present owners. The hall narrowed to a corridor leading to the drawing room and the dining room opposite and ultimately opening on to the garden. These principal reception rooms were an essay in pared-down neoclassicism, plain ceilings with deep dentil cornices being almost the only decoration. The drawing room opened into the smaller morning room, also accessible from the gallery running off the hall to the right. The panelled library (accessible from the drawing room) had a distinctly American feel to it, despite its English origins.

The library opened on to the porch, so the room was probably intended as the daily sitting room. Because it was set at a 45 degree angle to the other reception rooms there was room for a small library hall, with a telephone booth and a cloakroom, tucked in beneath the master bedroom staircase. Upstairs, aside from the master bedroom, there were a further five bedrooms, two dressing rooms, six bathrooms, a sewing and cleaning room, a children's room and a room for the governess. There were also seven maids' rooms and another two rooms on the ground floor for male servants.

The gardens were designed by two of the most prominent women landscape architects of the period, Ellen Biddle Shipman and Marian Cruger Coffin.[16] From Long Island they imported mature box to create a box garden beside the library. To shade the entrance porch they brought in yet more box, and also some large elms. More elms were brought in to shade the garden façade. (Sadly, all the elms are now long gone.) Further afield there were tennis courts, a swimming pool and perennial borders set in wide rolling lawns and woodlands.

In those years life for the Kinnicutts, as for other people of their class, had a set pattern and order. The family spent the winter in New York, then moved to Morristown – or later to Mayfields – on Maundy Thursday, the day before Good Friday. They left Mayfields for their house at Dark Harbor on the island of Isleboro in Maine on the Bar Harbor express on or near to 2 July, boarding the *J.T. Moss* at Rockland, Maine, for the short ferry journey: 'met at the dock by surreys and buckboards, we travelled around the harbor and through the pine woods to my grandparents' house on the point.'[17] They went back to Mayfields at the beginning of September, on the day after Labor Day, finally returning once more to New York on the Monday after Thanksgiving, just as autumn gave way to winter. This was the rhythm of life.

FAR LEFT The drawing room at Mayfields.

LEFT The corridor. Sister inherited the looking glass, which was one of a pair.

BELOW The library. The doors on the right opened on to the porch.

ABOVE One of the guest bedrooms, with twin American campaign beds.

BELOW Mrs Kinnicutt's bedroom. Sister was born in the four-poster bed.

RIGHT Mrs Kinnicutt's bureau in her bedroom. The carved wood valances ended up in the living room in Sister's Town House in Maine.

It was expected that girls would marry young, but first you had to 'come out'. Sister's coming-out party was held in New York during the Christmas holidays of 1927.[18] The next task was to find suitable beaux. Sister observed, 'I have found that girls who do poorly at school, and who can't fence, usually make up for it by having enormous success with boys' – but 'I cannot say that the theory proved true in my case.'[19] Her parents were not impressed by any of the young men Sister brought home; her mother became more than ever convinced that 'Yale was not really a college and that those who went there had little justification for being alive. She felt the same about Princeton.'[20] Whoever 'he' might be, he most certainly had to be from Harvard, and preferably a member of the elite Porcellian Club (membership of which had eluded even Franklin D. Roosevelt). May Kinnicutt decided that she had better take charge of the matter, so she arranged a dinner party where all the young men were at least three years out of Harvard and settled in good jobs either in banking or finance. Sister recalled that 'we girls were all in a state of excitement and dread, and I doubt that any of us would have said more than two intelligible words to the men if one of them hadn't been so polite that he saw his duty to make an effort with us.'[21] This was Harry Parish.

Henry Parish II (1903–1977), known throughout his life as Harry, was extremely good-looking, with bright blue eyes and broad shoulders. He was also, by common consent, a lovely person – kind, gentle and sweet-natured. The Parishes were an old New York family, related by marriage to many of the other great families, including the Roosevelts. Harry's uncle Henry Parish, after whom he was named, had married Eleanor Roosevelt's cousin Susan Ludlow Parish. It was really Susie who brought Eleanor up (Susie always said that had she known Eleanor would become First Lady she would have had her teeth straightened, and that she regretted not having had the foresight to do this).[22] The Parishes were also extremely rich, far richer than the Kinnicutts. Harry's father, Edward Parish, was a lawyer, and a very successful one, but the real wealth came from his grandfather, Henry Parish, who was the President of the New York Insurance & Trust Co., the oldest trust company in the United States.

It soon became clear that Sister and Harry were in love and that 'discussions' would need to take place between the two families. Mrs Parish arranged to meet Mrs Kinnicutt at the Tea Court of the Plaza Hotel. The discussions could have foundered before they even began, as Mrs Parish opened by announcing that her daughter was 'contemplating divorce', a shocking and shameful thing to have in any family. Fortunately the Kinnicutts were prepared to overlook such matters, as in every other way Harry was an entirely suitable young man. Harry and Sister were married on Valentine's Day 1930 at St George's Church near Gramercy Park in New York.

As part of her dowry, the Kinnicutts provided their daughter with a house at 146 East End Avenue, New York, and had it decorated from attic to cellar by Mrs Brown of McMillen's. Thus gainfully employed and comfortably housed they embarked upon married life. But the storms that would engulf and radically change their lives were in reality already upon them.

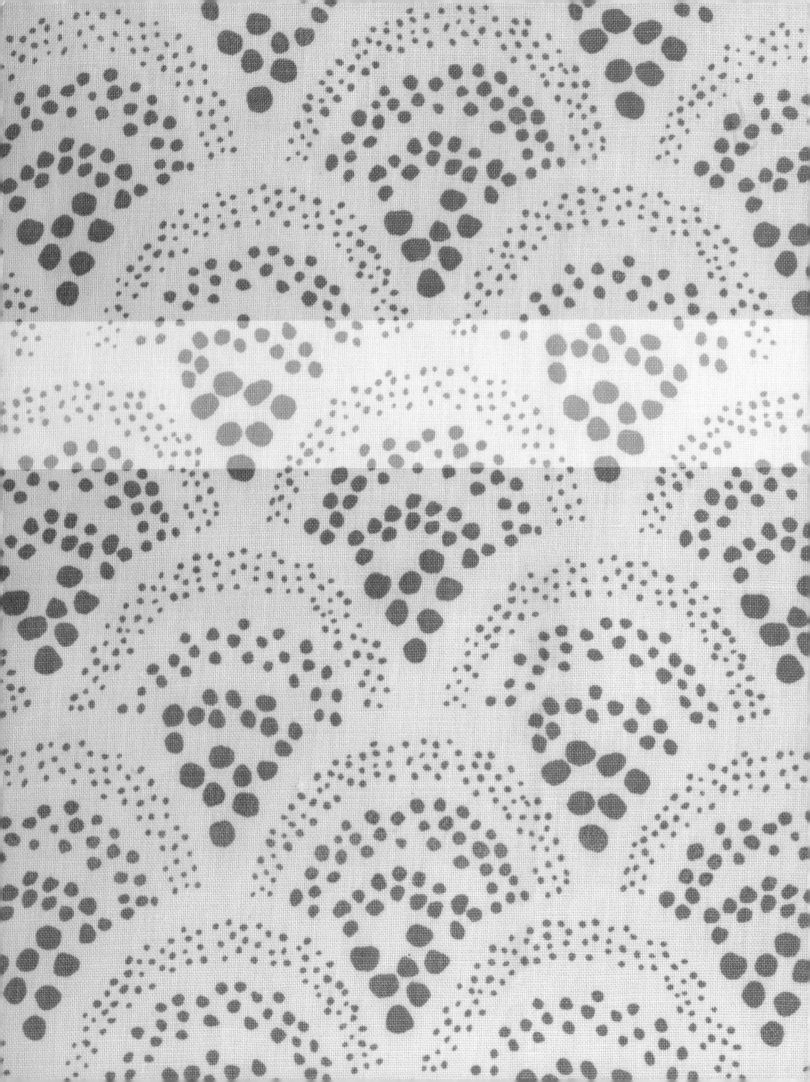

IN TRADE

Harry and Sister with their daughter D.B. in 1940. PREVIOUS PAGES Parish-Hadley 'Chou-Chou' in teal.

IN TRADE

I n the Wall Street Crash of 1929 the Kinnicutt and the Parish families, like so many others, lost huge amounts of money, in both capital and income. Nor, of course, was the crash a single event. The market actually bottomed on 8 July 1932, at which point it had lost 89 per cent of its value. It did not regain that value for over twenty years, actually reaching its pre-1929 level only on 23 November 1954.

Harry Parish worked for Rhoades & Co. (which in 1937 became Loeb, Rhoades & Co.), a New York firm of stockbrokers. The crash impacted heavily on their business and they cut the salaries of all their employees. It was clear that unless some additional source of income could be found the expenditure of the Parish household would have to be drastically pruned. Sister had no intention of reducing the style of life to which she was accustomed. There was only one thing she could do: work.

The Parishes' first child, Henry Parish III (Harry), was born in 1931. His first word was apparently 'birdie', which was taken to indicate a desire for country life. This was fortunate, as in 1932 his parents found and rented a small farmhouse in Far Hills, New Jersey, on Dunwalke, the estate of Clarence Dillon.[1] Sister decorated the house herself, and it was this modest enterprise that laid the foundations of her subsequent career. The white clapboard house, with its bright yellow shutters, was surrounded by apple trees, all contained within a white picket fence. The garden was filled with violets, and watercress grew in the stream that meandered across the property. Mrs Parish offered them some furniture, and Sister chose a suite of black ebony covered in blue tapestry with pink flowers. She painted it white. Harry's mother eventually conceded that the effect was 'interesting'. In the sitting room Sister mirrored one wall to reflect a white and brown striped wallpaper. A pair of white sofas, two white and gold console tables with marble tops, and a papier mâché table with a fringe furnished the room. White mattress ticking was used for the curtains (Mrs Parish wondered when the curtains would arrive). Thus Sister had her version of a 'white' room, à la Syrie Maugham.[2]

Shortly after moving in they decided that they would build a new master bedroom on the ground floor and link it to the sitting room with a greenhouse.

ABOVE The sitting room in the Far Hills farmhouse which the Parishes rented.

LEFT The farmhouse. The Parishes added the section on the right.

BELOW Sister and her daughters in the greenhouse.

ABOVE The Parish family – Apple, Sister, 'little Harry', D.B. and Harry – in the sitting room of the Far Hills house in 1940.

RIGHT The family in front of the house.

BELOW Sister's bedroom with the red and white painted floor.

BOTTOM Apple and D.B. by the sitting room fire.

Basically the greenhouse was a lean-to, with large windows to the ground but a solid roof rather than glass (which would have made it too hot in summer and too cold in winter). The floor was of old bricks. This room was furnished with a very deep sofa (an Aiken sofa) in yellow canvas, covered in lots of large squashy cushions, and there were also two white wicker chairs. Filled with terracotta pots of bulbs and geraniums, it became a delightful living room, while the old sitting room was used more as an evening room.

Beyond, they built their new bedroom. The room had a huge ceiling of the type known as a tray ceiling (that is, with a recessed centre). This, like the walls, was painted dead white. Sister painted the floor too, but with a pattern of squares in cherry red and white. (Poor Harry spent much of the summer marking out the squares to ensure they were exactly right.) The fireplace mantel was made from Steuben glass, but the mouldings were applied directly to the wall and painted the same red as the floor. Over the bed she created a corona in white silk taffeta, giving height and a sense of drama. 'I was so impressed', a friend recalled, 'when I went into this very bright bedroom that went right up to the eaves. She had all these pictures tied with little bows, and it was the first time I'd seen such a thing. First time anyone had. There were these enormous squares of lipstick red painted on the floor. Red and white. A beautiful bedroom, different than anything anyone had ever seen.'[3] These stylish interiors created quite a stir in the small community. Word got around and soon Sister found that her advice was being sought.

When the Essex Hunt Club asked her to rearrange their living room, she threw out the uncomfortable chairs and imported upholstered sofas and chairs, a daring thing to do in so conservative a club. On either side of the fireplace and across the top of the mantel she placed mirrors, creating a 'wall of mirrors' so people could see themselves dancing in their hunting pink and fine evening dresses. Improved lighting and a large coffee table, which she herself donated as a goodwill gesture, completed the effect. It was very well received. The next project was to revamp what had been the ballroom of the Dark Harbor Inn in Maine, a place she had known since childhood. This time she worked with her friend Phyllis Dillon. They used two shades of pink, pale on the walls and deeper on the rafters. The chairs were painted pale blue and the tables were a mixture with some pink and some blue. This was probably not her finest job.

Interior decorators were then a comparatively new species. The trade basically grew out of antique dealing and upholstery firms. In the eighteenth century, on both sides of the Atlantic, in decoration the upholsterer usually held sway. As he supplied many of the most expensive components in a house, it was quite natural that he would be supreme. The upholsterer would expand and other trades would join him, and some of these firms continued into the nineteenth century and on into the twentieth. In London Morants, or Lenygon and Morant as they became, were one example and Keebles another, while Herter Brothers in New York followed a similar pattern. Elsie de Wolf (Lady Mendl) made her fortune as an antique dealer, buying furniture for Henry Frick, and this led her into decoration. Sibyl Colefax began decorating professionally just before Sister, taking over the failing decorating department of the antique dealers Stair and Andrew in Bruton Street, Mayfair. But Sister set out as a decorator.

In the winter of 1933, without telling her husband, she went to see the president of Stroheim and Romann in the Decorators' Building in New York. As a result of her sheer persistence (one rather suspects at least in part as a way of getting rid of this troublesome woman), he gave her a trade account, and even helped her to a waiting taxi with bundles of samples. She did the same thing at Johnson & Faulkner (now Joffre), with similar results.[4] She then found a small room in the old L.V. Ludlow & Co. building in Far Hills, adjacent to the saddler's, for the modest rent of $35 a month.[5]

The room Sister rented was tiny, only 14 feet square, and she picked up a paint brush herself to do out the whole shop in white. She opened her business on the Wednesday after Christmas Day 1933. That first morning, armed with a piece of paper, a pencil, a wicker chair and a wicker table, together with all the samples she had brought from Stroheim's and Johnson & Faulkner, she was in business.

At this point she plucked up the courage to confess to her husband (when he first saw the shop he somehow missed the sign outside in Sister's own handwriting announcing 'Mrs Henry Parish II, Interiors'). He had his reservations but finally approved. Some members of his family were not so understanding. When Harry's uncle Henry Parish and his wife, Susie, heard Sister had 'gone into trade' they promptly disinherited Harry, leaving a sizeable fortune to Eleanor Roosevelt. Even a Democrat was a more suitable recipient for the family fortune than a lady in trade.

It was a brave act to start out in business in the depths of so severe a depression, but in this instance it would seem that fortune did indeed favour the bold. Business must have been steady from very early on, because Sister was soon employing a lady from the nearby hotel as her bookkeeper. Although she had no formal training, she knew almost by instinct how to arrange furniture, and she had a natural feeling for colour. About the only thing she needed to do was some research on pelmet designs. Basically she seems to have copied a selection from books and these became her stock designs.

In writing about those times Sister mentions her first major client, Mrs Anderson Fowler (the former Miss Genevieve Brady), a family friend, who, on her marriage in 1937, had a large country house to decorate and a $100,000 budget with which to do it.[6] The house, Glenelg in Peapack, New Jersey, had been built by her husband's father in 1907. It was designed by the architect Edward Shepard Hewitt, who also made later additions when he was in partnership with the classical architect William Bottomley. Ogden Codman, famous for the book *The Decoration of Houses*, published in 1897 and written in collaboration with Edith Wharton, designed further features and also created a new staircase. As Sister recalled, 'I really didn't know much more than [the client] did, but she trusted me completely. I decided that they should have a dark green leather library and a white carpet with red roses. It was considered dashing.' It also got her and her work noticed and talked about.[7] Possibly it was Sister who mirrored the drawing room chimney breast wall, a trick she had already used at the Essex Hunt Club and in her own drawing room.

Sister also had some rather less upmarket commissions. In her recollections she mentions that a neighbour in Far Hills, Senator Frelinghuysen, approached her about a new restaurant in Somerville Circle, which badly needed some help with decoration. He introduced her to the owner, a Mr Hargraves. This restaurant was part of the Howard Johnson's chain, an early example of franchising.[8] The Howard Johnson's buildings were usually white clapboard, with dormers and a cupola, all resplendent under an eye-catching orange roof. Sister did this place in aqua – the walls were aqua, the placemats were aqua and the staff were dressed in aqua. In her memoirs she implies that the job, undertaken around 1938, was done merely for gallons of ice cream, but it would seem more likely that it was a proper commission.

On 7 December 1941 the world as the Parishes knew it came to an abrupt end, with the attack on Pearl Harbor and the declaration of war. Harry joined the navy, and Sister decided to close her business. She also closed up the farmhouse and went with her children to stay with her mother at Mayfields. After his initial training Harry was posted to various ships, and then to the Jacksonville naval base in Florida. He took a house outside the base and sent for his family. They lived there for over a year until his ship,

LEFT A screen Sister had covered
with old French botanical prints
and panelled antique paper for
Mrs Sheldon Prentice's New York
apartment.

RIGHT A cartoon of Sister that
appeared in a newspaper in the early
1960s, when she was one of the
decorators commissioned to create
table settings for Tiffany.

the light carrier USS *San Jacinto*, was commissioned on 15 December 1943. After the *San Jacinto* sailed for the Pacific Sister returned once more to New York, taking an apartment on East 82nd Street. Basic housekeeping was not her forte: her daughter recalls that on one occasion her mother cooked a ham rather too long, necessitating a visit from the New York Fire Department. Wisely deciding she had better stick to what she knew, with 'a couple of friends' from Far Hills she set up Budget Decorators. They were probably based on East 69th Street, but who the friends were no one now seems to recall.[9] It soon became apparent that Sister was doing all the work, so after a little more than a year she took back her own name and moved across the road to 22 East 69th Street. Here she was to remain for the next thirty years, only moving office to 305 East 63rd Street in 1980.

Sister worked hard during the last years of the war, doing up innumerable New York apartments and houses on Long Island and in upstate New York. As she recalled, 'I suppose that the rooms I decorated during those terrible years all looked pretty much alike. I still had limited knowledge, and of course it was a time of scarcity and austerity. However, I did know the words comfort and color.

And I did know how to make a room work.'[10] Her clients understood and appreciated what she was doing, and this proved to be the foundation of her post-war business.

During this period most of her work was for friends and friends of friends, and none of it was ever published. Nor, apparently, did Sister ever talk about her work at home. She was really creating rooms that were 'proper', 'genteel' – in what John Betjeman might have described as 'ghastly good taste'. These safe but dull interiors were what so many decorators, particularly 'lady decorators', had produced during the 1930s. They all to a greater or lesser extent reflect the Regency revival, with petite chairs and careful swags. Sister's own home is an example of this fashion.

After the war things began to change. Unlike most decorators, Sister does not seem to have courted publicity, at least at this point, but there were some mentions of her and her work in the press and magazines. The decorator Mark Hampton, who later worked for Sister at Parish-Hadley, was an avid reader of *Vogue* and *House & Garden* as a child in rural Indiana, and he recalled 'three photographs of Mrs Parish's work. These were of her Sutton Place apartment . . . a very modernistic, and uncharacteristic,

LEFT The Taliaferro house at Oyster Bay. The vaulted ceiling in the hall gave an illusion of height, while the diamond-patterned parquet floor running through both hall and drawing room made the whole appear more spacious. The small Directoire sofa was covered in coral-coloured silk.

BELOW LEFT The drawing room at Oyster Bay, with a pretty Italian chandelier and louvred shutters, was in faded greens and corals set against off-white walls.

BELOW RIGHT The drawing room of the Taliaferros' house in Old Brookville. Off-white walls contrasted with a light brown carpet and accents in pink and faded greens.

mirrored dining room for Mr and Mrs Laurence Rockefeller; and a beach house in Southampton for the daughter of Mrs Diego Suarez (Mr Suarez had designed the house).'[11] A screen designed for Mrs Sheldon Prentice's New York apartment was illustrated in *Vogue* in April 1950. Sister's own apartment at 4 Sutton Place was photographed for *Vogue*, appearing in the March 1951 issue in a piece on 'Eating all over the House'. The dining room she decorated for Winthrop Rockefeller (not Laurence Rockefeller) also appeared in *Vogue*, resplendent with antique mirrors reflecting ferns. Sister was becoming better known, and she was one of the decorators who were invited to create table settings by Tiffany in the early 1960s.

Among the houses that were published she was particularly proud of two, both for the same client. Charles Champe Taliaferro was a test pilot and famed aviator. He and his wife, Margaret (the former Margaret Savage), divided their time between Long Island, where Charles Taliaferro's aviation interests were based, and a winter residence in Hobe Sound, Florida. The two houses Sister decorated for them were both on Long Island. The first, in Old Brookville, although described in the *Vogue* article as 'English Regency', could almost have been in Provence. It was set on a hill, surrounded by tall trees, with a terrace opening on to rolling lawns, and the façade was washed in a delicious pinky-beige. This colour scheme was picked up inside, where the drawing room had off-white walls, a light beige-brown rug, and deeper-toned brown curtains. A sofa in a fern chintz from Brunschwig & Fils (still produced today) lifted the room, and some of the formal French provincial fruitwood furniture was upholstered in soft pink. Small tables with marbleized tops and bits of old lacquer completed the scheme. To all of this Mrs Taliaferro added masses of flowers in old painted tole containers and smaller specimens in crystal brandy glasses.

Soon after the house was finished the Taliaferros moved to Oyster Bay, to a small house designed for them by the architect Frederick King. He produced a charming

one-storey essay in pared-down Palladianism – a central block flanked by two supporting wings. In this house Sister experimented with a few radical ideas. In the hall and drawing room (in the main block of the house) she bleached the floor, a rather risky strategy as the end result can be a bit blotchy, giving a piebald look. Sister and Margaret Taliaferro were both nervous as the bleach was applied, but in the end the floor bleached beautifully. They then stained the floor with a diamond pattern, running from the hall through into the drawing room. The hall had a vaulted ceiling to give an illusion of height and had the same off-white walls as the drawing room beyond, its entrance guarded by a pair of blackamoors. The furniture seems mostly to have consisted of small French provincial pieces, such as a small secretaire and a Directoire sofa covered in coral-coloured silk. The off-white of the drawing room walls was broken by grisaille panelling done by Henry Billings. The colour scheme was planned around the fern chintz previously used in the house in Old Brookville, with accents of coral on other pieces. The curtains were of honey-coloured taffeta and were left unlined 'so they blew through the working shutters and made that rustling sound that only taffeta can make'.[12] One of the two wings was for the children, and formed a sort of self-contained annexe. The other wing contained the small library/dining room with the same off-white walls, coupled with pink marble and grey-greens. Through a wide pillared opening lay the sunroom. In the library, sunroom and bedrooms Sister and Margaret Taliaferro tried another experiment. 'We pasted vinyl white wall covering on the floors. The pattern was large squares. It lasted for years and years, to the wonderment of all.'[13] Apparently it was cared for with a damp mop and monthly waxing.

Over the years Sister worked extensively for Brooke Astor, Mrs Vincent Astor (they had known one another as children in Morristown).[14] An early commission was to work on the new house the Astors had created at Ferncliff in Rhinebeck, New York State. The original house, built by the Astors in the nineteenth century, was enormous. In 1903 Mrs John Jacob Astor commissioned the architect Stanford White to add a sports complex in the Beaux Arts style. Just after the Second World War Vincent Astor's second wife, Minnie (Mary Benedict Cushing), persuaded him to demolish the original house and to convert the sports annexe into a residence.

Third wife Brooke Astor didn't think much of this decision, remarking, 'I can't imagine a house where you came in the front door into a hall that ran straight through and looked out on the river – to tear that down and live in an old swimming pool house which didn't have one view.'[15] It was the 'old swimming pool house', now known as Astor Courts, that she set about redecorating in late 1953. Van Day Truex, that great 'arbiter of American taste', and Billy Baldwin, at the time the leading American decorator, both worked on this job, but Brooke turned for assistance to Sister as well.

The large entrance hall/sitting room, probably designed by Stanford White as a reception room, was lit by a huge skylight and had several large fan-topped French doors. It resembled a palm court from some grand Edwardian hotel. Sister copied the curtains he designed and retained much of the furniture that had originally stood in the room. With help from Van Day Truex, Brooke and Sister then converted two former squash courts to form a large library, a flower room and some storage space. Painted a pale grey with yellow curtains, and with a large rug especially designed for the room by Truex in a contemporary abstract pattern, the library made a comfortable everyday sitting room.[16]

The guest rooms were filled with furniture from the former mansion and probably contained fittings salvaged from that house. In Brooke Astor's bedroom stood a *lit à la polonaise* that eventually found its way to her New York apartment. Here French doors opened on to a veranda, the large windows flooding the room with light and afternoon sunshine. Painted off-white, the bed was hung with a rose-patterned chintz also used for the curtains, with their festoon draperies – which don't appear hugely successful – and for loose covers. The annexe also contained one of the first private indoor swimming pools in the United States, which Brooke separated off with glass doors. Some 60 × 24 feet, it had a glass roof and a wall of glass. Brooke Astor (who always liked pools on the warm side) and Sister filled the space with comfortable sofas and plenty of plants.

Sister also worked for Vincent Astor's first wife, Helen Dinsmore Huntington (described, somewhat scurrilously and probably also inaccurately, by the novelist Glenway Wescott as a 'grand, old-fashioned lesbian'). Her second husband was the real estate broker Lytle Hull. In the early 1940s she inherited The Locusts, which had been her grandfather's house, from an aunt. Originally built in 1873 and known as Dinsmore Place, the house was hopelessly impractical, so Helen had it demolished and commissioned a new, more compact house from the architect John Churchill. He created a pleasant neo-baroque house, which was stuccoed and washed a pale blue. To take advantage of the delightful views over the Hudson Valley, Churchill built the house on a slightly concave plan with a large drawing room at one end and a smaller dining room at the other.

Helen Hull had a lot of pretty things to go in her new house, including an eighteenth-century Bessarabian rug that was used in the drawing room, a large room which ran the full width of the house. The rug's muted tones provided the key for the decoration: a preponderance of soft colours, fresh lettuce green, soft mauve, pink and yellow, with a sharp highlight from a pair of crimson silk armchairs. These were later reupholstered in chintz, but that aside the room remained unchanged for the next thirty years. The dining room at the opposite end of the house was dominated by a Georgian triple pillar dining table. This room was treated quite simply. One unusual feature was a niche with brackets of varying sizes, created to display part of Mrs Hull's fine collection of porcelain. On the opposite wall a companion niche was created in *trompe l'oeil*. An Indian silk rug and blue silk curtains completed the effect.

Helen Hull was a prominent figure on the New York social scene and a great supporter of the musical life of the city, being on the board of the Metropolitan Opera, the New York City Ballet and the New York Philharmonic Society. She was also a gifted pianist and The Locusts was often filled with musicians. After Helen Hull died in 1976 the house was featured in *Architectural Digest*. Sister's name was not mentioned and the decoration was credited to Nanny Tiffany; however, most of the work was Sister's.

Although Sister always insisted that she was not greatly interested in architecture, she did understand houses, how a house should fit in its setting and how it should work from a practical point of view. This talent came into its own in a commission of 1956. Visiting a friend in Boston, Sister was taken to dinner at the house of Thomas Jefferson Coolidge in Brookline, a suburb of Boston. Coolidge, a member of an old Boston family, was a banker who had also served as under-secretary of the treasury under President Roosevelt. At dinner his wife, Catherine, asked Sister if she liked the dining room, adding, 'I find something lacking.' This is always a tricky question for a decorator to answer, but, choosing to be direct, Sister replied, 'I'm afraid everything is the matter.'

Much to her surprise, a year later Catherine Coolidge telephoned and asked if she would look at a model and some plans prepared by the architect Page Cross[17] for a new house to be built at Coolidge Point, Massachusetts, to replace the 'marble palace' built for the family in the early 1900s by the New York architects McKim, Mead and White – Stanford White's old practice. To say Sister was underwhelmed by the model for the new house was an understatement: 'It looked

LEFT Helen Dinsmore Huntington, shortly before her marriage to Vincent Astor in 1914.

ABOVE RIGHT The drawing room of The Locusts, decorated by Sister just after the Second World War.

BELOW RIGHT The master bedroom at The Locusts.

BELOW FAR RIGHT The dining room. The niche was created to display Mrs Hull's porcelain.

like Uncle Tom's cabin without the outhouse! . . . "We want something small and practical," Jeff said. "Something we can run ourselves." . . . Fortunately, Jeff began to laugh before I could issue any comment. Even Jeff, who was the most careful of Bostonians, could not see his lavish Catherine or himself squeezed into the space indicated by the model in his hands.'[18] The architect's instructions were revised, much to his relief. Eventually what he created – with, it appears, a good deal of help and advice from Sister – resembled three low pavilions linked together. As Sister recalled, 'What it finally became was a very big little house. The rooms kept getting bigger and bigger, and there were always more bedrooms.'[19]

A lightly wooded promontory surrounded by the chilly blue waters of the Atlantic on three sides, the site for the new house was beautiful and dramatic. Cross rather cleverly did not set the house four-square to the ocean, but turned it, setting it further back than the 'marble palace' had stood in order to allow views of the coves along the shoreline as it stretched into the distance. The round entrance hall was basically created to house a collection of portraits by Gilbert Stuart of the first five presidents of the United States. These portraits had hung in the dining room of the Brookline house, but Catherine Coolidge decided she had had quite enough of those 'old men staring at me while I'm eating'.[20] The room could have looked a bit like an art gallery, but this effect was modified by the impact of a small raised lyre-shaped fireplace, a most unusual design. The floor was unpolished pink marble and the walls were

done in a pale sand colour. Not everyone was impressed. The great connoisseur of American decoration Henry du Pont (with whom Sister was to work at the White House) confidently pronounced: 'This room is too small for these portraits' – only to be told by Catherine Coolidge that 'Any room is too small for five presidents!'[21] Turning left you came to the dining room, with an apricot marbleized table on a gilded baroque base, surrounded by faux bamboo chairs, all of which Sister had made for the house in her New York workrooms. A right turn led you into the drawing room and the trellis room beyond.

The Coolidges wanted a house that was light and lively – a complete contrast to their Brookline house – and this was what Sister sought to achieve, particularly in the drawing room, which was flooded with light from the enormous bay window, some 18 feet long, with views across the lawns to the ocean beyond. Unusually, the windows had working shutters, all of which had to be handmade. The floor was painted in off-white and brown scallops, with the outline of each scallop incised. The painter Louis Perry applied numerous coats of paint and must have spent

ABOVE Mrs Coolidge's bedroom in the Coolidge Point house,

FAR LEFT The dining room, with the marbleized table and faux bamboo chairs Sister had made.

LEFT The sunny sitting room known as the trellis room.

RIGHT The drawing room.

weeks on his knees. A fine nineteenth-century Oushak rug anchored the room but left a 7-foot edge of painted floor. The soft colours of the rug – pale yellow, tangerine, light blue, and a pale sand colour – seemed to reflect the colours of the landscape, and the colour scheme continued with the walls, which were dragged and glazed in a very pale yellow. The upholstery was in corn colour and pale corals, plus stinging greens. A 9-foot armoire painted off-white lived happily with chinoiserie Chippendale mirrors, gilt console tables, and lacquer pieces arranged around the room. It was a skilful mix of French and English. Sadly, Thomas Jefferson Coolidge died just two weeks before they were due to move in, but his widow lived there happily for the rest of her life. After she died the family gave most of the land to the Trustees of Reservations.[22] The house was demolished in 1989.

Country houses tend to be more interesting and much more fun for a decorator than city apartments, but it is the latter that usually provide the bread and butter of the business. Sister's business was no exception, and she did many such apartments. One example was the town house for Bennett Cerf, the founder of the publishers Random House, which was unusual in that the dining room was combined with the office. Shutters could be closed to conceal the desk, or, when there was a large party, the desk could double as the buffet. It still looks surprisingly modern.

In Washington, D.C., Sister decorated the Victorian townhouse of Mrs Oates Leiter at 3259 R Street, not far from Dumbarton Oaks. Once the home of the illustrator William Dougal, the house had remained in the Dougal family until it was bought by Mr and Mrs Robert Leiter in 1959. The story goes that 'Oatsie' Leiter struggled with the house until Lily Guest told her quite firmly 'Stop all of this nonsense and call up Sister Parish,' which she then did. The drawing room, as decorated by Sister, was illustrated in *The Finest Rooms*, a selection of work from America's greatest

ABOVE LEFT The drawing room at Coolidge Point. Its wide bay windows opened on to glorious views towards the ocean.

ABOVE RIGHT Catherine Coolidge's bathroom, which was laid out as a comfortable sitting room.

BELOW RIGHT The dining room of Bennett Cerf's New York house.

BELOW FAR RIGHT Bennett Cerf's desk doubled as a buffet.

decorators published in 1964. South-facing, with a huge bay window overlooking R Street and two French windows on to the garden, the room was bright and light. In keeping with the Victorian architecture, the decoration had a distinctly Victorian air. The two deep-buttoned low-backed sofas were upholstered in crimson silk damask, a colour picked up by the curtains and the swag and tail draperies. This deep red (which helped absorb some of the abundant natural light) was echoed by the Aubusson carpet, which also supplied the accent colour, a gold silk used on the suite of French chairs.

The decoration remained unchanged, except in minor details, for the next fifty years. The gold silk upholstery on the French chairs was replaced by cream silk with a bright check pattern on the back of the chairs and the skirted table got a new cloth, but the crimson sofas remained, as did their companion curtains. Oatsie Leiter, or Oatsie Charles as she became, finally sold the house in October 2008. In the course of the intervening fifty years virtually anyone who was anyone, or had pretensions to be anyone, on the Washington social scene had passed through her drawing room, including a succession of presidents. It was here that President Kennedy met Ian Fleming. The Leiters were friends of Fleming and the character Felix Leiter in the Bond novels is named after them.

While Sister was working on the decoration of R Street, she began to redecorate a house just down the road. This was the job that was to make her a household name.

The drawing room at 3259 R Street, decorated for Oatsie Leiter.

IN SEARCH
OF STYLE

The garden façade of Ditchley Park, Oxfordshire, in 1948. **PREVIOUS PAGES** Parish-Hadley 'Burma' in willow.

IN SEARCH OF STYLE

Although Sister always claimed that her childhood visits to Europe left her untouched, it was a different story when she had grown up a little. She described a visit to Paris in 1928, when she was eighteen, as a turning point. Wandering from room to room at her parents' apartment at 23 Quai d'Orsay, 'I marvelled at the carved fruitwood tables, Aubusson carpets, and painted furniture. I was discovering something I knew was important, though I couldn't have said why.'[1] The following summer she, along with the rest of her family, returned to Paris. By this time she was engaged to Henry Parish and preoccupied. She concentrated on buying 'small flower drawings, old teacups, and beribboned porcelain bowls for "our" house'.[2]

After the Wall Street Crash, through the long years of the Depression and the Second World War, there were few opportunities for foreign travel until 1948, when Sister came to England to discuss a business arrangement with Colefax and Fowler, the London decorators owned by Nancy Lancaster. She sailed with her friend Mrs Paul ('Bunny') Mellon, probably on the *Queen Mary*. An abiding memory of that time was a visit to Ditchley Park in Oxfordshire, the home of Ronald Tree. By this time Ronnie was divorced from his first wife, Nancy. He had married Marietta Peabody and Nancy was married to Colonel Claude Lancaster. But what impressed Sister was the beauty of the rooms created during Nancy's time as chatelaine of Ditchley.

Sister wrote to her husband on her first morning, and her enthusiasm flowed faster than her pen across the page: 'Ronnie and Marietta opened the door and in I walked to the most fantastically beautiful house that I have ever hoped to see . . . . Room after room of such pieces, the way they are placed, the needlework carpets, crystal chandeliers – all candles, china – Oh Lord, it's terrific.' As Sister toured the house her enthusiasm built; she found each successive room 'more perfect than the last. A good deal of the furniture was here from when it was built in 1725. The bedrooms are even better if possible. All four-poster beds with crowned tops. In my room now I had to get on a little stepladder (covered in white damask) to get up. The furniture is white lacquer with green jade! Each bath has a fireplace and such gems as needlework bath mats, beautiful consols (as sinks), baskets of toilet paper with lavender bags – I could go on forever, but I have no power of description.'

A watercolour painting by
Alexandre Serebriakoff of the Great
Hall at Ditchley, as it was in 1948.

Tea was served in the Great Hall – pale blue walls with
red and white upholstery and pictures by William Kent – and
then dinner in the large dining room, the candles burning
in the chandelier and Russian crystal wall sconces glowing
against the pale grey walls, 'fresh asparagus, four glasses of
one thing after another, just the boys and the D'Elangers –
great fun and laughter – bed at one . . . looking down from
my bed now in every direction vistas of trees. One vista is of
chestnut trees (in full bloom), then elms, then beech. A box-
wood garden with lime tree hedges – sheep are roaming the
pastures and deer the park!'[3]

Nancy Lancaster (1897–1994) was described as having
'the finest taste of anyone in the world', but she was never
a decorator in the accepted sense of the word: indeed she
said herself that she was 'agin decorating', describing herself
rather as 'a percolator of ideas'. It was the way the percolator
worked and the quality of the result that was so special.
And there was also perhaps something else. That was an
infectious love of life, a generosity and warmth allied to a
great talent for living, which Nancy infused into the very
fabric of her houses. As a guest at Ditchley you felt the
warmth of the welcome. Nancy and Ronnie were always

 **ABOVE LEFT** The Orange Bedroom, which Sister occupied during her stay at Ditchley. The *lit à la polonaise* was hung with parchment-coloured silk taffeta.

TOP RIGHT The dressing table bedecked with muslin, typical of Nancy Lancaster's style.

ABOVE RIGHT The orange and white Mauny wallpaper, printed in France in the 1930s.

delighted to see you: they were desolate when you took your leave (or seemed so). The decoration of Ditchley was a partnership. Ronnie bought the pictures and some of the grand furniture, but it was Nancy who chose the fabrics and arranged the house.

In 1944, towards the end of her marriage with Ronnie, Nancy bought the firm of Colefax and Fowler from its founder, Sibyl Colefax.[4] Along with the stock she acquired John Fowler, and so one of the most creative decorative partnerships of the twentieth century was born. By the time John Fowler went into partnership with Lady Colefax in 1938

he was already recognized as one of the leading decorators of the period. After the war, in partnership with Nancy, he dominated fashionable taste.

Writing years later, Sister recalled, 'When I think of John, I think of impossibly detailed curtains with dressmaker furbelows, and of rooms that are romantic without being sentimental or bitsy, a look that is very difficult to achieve.'[5] What appealed to Sister about John Fowler's work was its very Englishness, just like the man himself, who, she found, 'was unassuming – as English as Billy Baldwin was American'.

John Fowler (1906–1977), the 'Prince of Decorators', in the garden of his country house, the Hunting Lodge, in the 1950s.

It was probably through Nancy that Sister met John Fowler. John's diary reveals that on Tuesday 30 March 1948 he was 'very busy at Brook St arranging for Mrs Parish'. She arrived on Friday 2 April: 'Mrs Parish from New York to buy: lunch Nancy.' On Thursday 8 April, 'Nancy, Sister P., Lady Salisbury and I motored to Hatfield. Lunched with the Cranbornes. Hitchen after.' Aside from all the gallivanting there was a business purpose to Sister's visit. At the time rationing made it impossible for Colefax and Fowler to obtain trimmings. Sister came armed with a proposition: she would send trims over from the United States, and Colefax and Fowler would supply her with antiques for her clients. It was envisioned as a mutually beneficial arrangement. A deal was struck and the following week there were drinks at Nancy's before Sister departed. The deal actually soon came to grief on account of currency restrictions, but a link had been forged.

She returned to England in October and John records, rather drily, 'Wednesday 13 October: Sister expected but didn't turn up.' She did appear the following day. These visits continued over the years and Sister would also quite often go to John's house, the Hunting Lodge, usually to lunch. In 1954, her brief and disastrous marriage to Colonel Lancaster at an end, Nancy bought Haseley Court in Oxfordshire. If any house fired Sister's imagination it was surely this, the most beautiful of all Nancy's houses. She was a frequent guest, usually staying for the weekend during her visits to England, often with her husband, occasionally with Albert Hadley.[6] What impressed Sister was not only Nancy's sense of style, but also her wit: she noted how, at Haseley, 'Nancy sat at one end of the dining room in a Queen Anne wing chair, slip-covered in chintz and with pillows thrown in its hollows. Except for the man sitting opposite in a chair that was the twin to hers, all the other guests were given tufted William IV leather ones. I always found the contrast amusing.'

The drawing room at Cornbury Park
in Oxfordshire, one of the last private
rooms decorated by John Fowler. The
curtains, with their intricate draperies,
were some of the most elaborate he
ever created.

BELOW The Blue Room at Colefax and Fowler, which was later to become Nancy's bedroom. The furnishings included paired Regency waterfall display shelves, early nineteenth-century neoclassical pier glasses, and Chinese reverse glass portraits.

BOTTOM The room which was to become Nancy's Yellow Room, a photograph taken while it was in use as a showroom in 1948.

RIGHT The showrooms of Sibyl Colefax and John Fowler Ltd, 39 Brook Street, Mayfair, in 1950.

BELOW RIGHT A panelled showroom at Colefax and Fowler, with a pair of eighteenth-century painted side chairs, a late eighteenth-century *bonheur de jour* and, displayed on the walls, an early nineteenth-century English dessert service.

OPPOSITE ABOVE A gothic bookcase which Bunny Mellon bought from Colefax and Fowler when she visited London with Sister in 1948.

OPPOSITE RIGHT The North Room at Colefax and Fowler in 1948. The nineteenth-century giltwood corner sofas are very much in the Colefax and Fowler style.

OPPOSITE FAR RIGHT A selection of pieces from Colefax and Fowler's stock, including a late eighteenth-century painted side table with inlaid marble top, and a pair of eighteenth-century side chairs.

ABOVE LEFT The saloon at Haseley Court in Nancy's time was a freewheeling mix of the formal and informal.

LEFT Another view of the saloon.

ABOVE The north-west face of Haseley Court, overlooking the famous chess set.

RIGHT The dining room, where Nancy used Queen Anne wing chairs as carvers.

The core of Haseley is a small Queen Anne manor house built around 1704 on the site of a medieval hall house, a fragment of which remains. In the mid-eighteenth century two wings were added, one containing a saloon or drawing room in the neoclassical style, and the other a gothic library. Unlike Nancy's other great houses – Mirador in Virginia, Kelmarsh and Ditchley in England – Haseley was a mixture of styles rather than a uniform whole. And yet the house was wonderfully harmonious. When Nancy bought Haseley, it was a wreck. She and John Fowler set to work. As John later explained, what was significant was 'not only what was done but what was not done. Chintzes and silks were freely mixed; and there was an avoidance of materials and colours matching and of sets of furniture that would give a

static character, or indeed of a "period" feeling . . . And yet none of the original decoration . . . was disturbed. Indeed at Haseley the plasterwork was most carefully restored. Thus history was respected but reinterpreted to meet the needs and tastes of a particular person.'[7] Nancy was that person. This gave the house vitality and life. It also gave quite formal rooms a degree of informality, which was one of the hallmarks of the house.

Of the many rooms created by John and Nancy, two, in particular, were exceptional. One of these was Nancy's bedroom in the old medieval part of Haseley. Playing on the 'gothic' theme, Nancy added a cornice copied from one at St Michael's Mount in Cornwall. Then she had John Fowler and master craftsman George Oakes paint *trompe l'oeil* 'stucco' details on the walls and ceiling. The point of *trompe l'oeil* is not that it closely imitates but that it momentarily deceives, and in this room the 'trick of the eye' succeeds superbly. The room is a spectacular tour de force. It was furnished with an odd assortment of objects, so much so that it could almost have resembled a disorderly antique dealer's shop. And yet it seems to have a natural harmony.

At around the same time as they decorated the Gothic Bedroom, Nancy and John created another astonishing room – one that Sister came to know extremely well. This was the reception room in Nancy's London apartment above the Colefax and Fowler Mayfair showrooms. When Nancy took the apartment over, in 1957, this room was decorated in grey-green and white, which she thought far too cold.

LEFT The Gothic Bedroom at Haseley.

ABOVE RIGHT Above the fireplace in the Gothic Bedroom was a *trompe l'oeil* medallion of the goddess Diana painted by John Fowler and George Oakes. Nancy complained that it revealed their lack of understanding of female anatomy.

BELOW RIGHT The bathroom of the Gothic Bedroom, with its huge decagonal window. Nancy always laid out her bathrooms like charming sitting rooms.

ABOVE The Tobacco Bedroom, at
Haseley Court, hung with an old
French wallpaper portraying –
appropriately, in a house owned by
a Virginian – the tale of *Paul et Virginie*.

RIGHT The famous Yellow Room in
Nancy's apartment above the
Colefax and Fowler showrooms.

Nancy on the steps of Haseley Court
in the mid-1960s.

She decided to paint it a deep golden yellow and to glaze the surface so that it was very glossy and reflective. Numerous coats of paint were applied; then John 'spent hours with the layers of glaze'. No one knows exactly what he did, and it has proved impossible to recreate the effect. But the result was a room that shimmered with light. John then added very theatrical curtains which he had made from yellow silk taffeta and shantung, hanging them from thick gilded rods adorned with yards of silken cord and big tassels.

The houses designed by Nancy and John had a huge influence on Sister. Her business partner, Albert Hadley, remarked that Nancy's style 'reminded me of life in Tennessee where people had lived in houses for generations. It was what I call "dilapidated elegance".' He could see what Nancy was doing, but it didn't influence him as much as it did Sister. 'It wasn't as if it was decoration at all; it was the way a house evolves. The way houses that are lived in and loved take on personality and an ambience and the character of the inhabitants.' To Albert Nancy was the 'most fascinating woman I have ever met' and it was interesting to watch and observe her and Sister together. 'Sis had a quiet manner about her and spoke very softly, with a very keen sense of humour, and sometimes a slightly wicked tongue,' whereas Nancy 'was the absolute opposite. She never stopped talking, in quite a loud voice, and never sat down. And Sis was always lying down, or as near lying down as she could get in polite society.'[8]

Sister was also good at allowing a house to evolve, but she was looking for something more: a style that was her own. She found it almost by accident. In January 1967 *House & Garden* magazine published an article on Sister's house in Maine. It caused a sensation. The style was what we now call the American Country Style and in many ways it was an invention of Sister's – or, at any rate, it was she who developed it into something distinctive.

The sitting room of the Coach House
at Haseley, Nancy's home for the last
twenty years of her life.

DECORATING CAMELOT

President and Mrs Kennedy in the Yellow Oval Room in early 1963. **PREVIOUS PAGES** Parish-Hadley 'Kinnicutt' in red.

DECORATING CAMELOT

On 20 January 1961 John Fitzgerald Kennedy was inaugurated as the 35th President of the United States. Following his narrow election victory over Richard Nixon on 8 November 1960, Kennedy's wife, Jacqueline, had begun to look at the White House, her new home, and she was frankly unimpressed with what she found. It seemed natural to her to turn to Sister Parish for help with the restoration and redecoration of the most iconic building in America. Others, however, were somewhat puzzled. The *New York Times* ran a headline proclaiming 'Kennedys select nun to decorate White House'. Soon, though, Sister's work on the White House had made her a household name across the United States.

Sister had met Jacqueline Kennedy in the early spring of 1960 when Jackie sought advice on decorating a cottage on the Kennedy estate at Hyannis Point. Sister worked her magic, filling the Kennedy sitting room with 'flower chintz, straw rugs, a hooked rug, new Staffordshire lamps, lots of different patterned pillows. With the flowers and the earthenware pots and the woven baskets, a knitted wool blanket to tuck under her chin, and a fire burning, Jackie now had a room that could be cheerful and cosy on those foggy Hyannis nights.'[1]

Pleased with her pretty room, Jackie then asked Sister to look at her Washington house at 3307 N Street in Georgetown. Jackie had originally wanted Stéphane Boudin of the Parisian firm of Jansen to decorate the Georgetown house,[2] but he was beyond even her budget, so she employed her sister, Lee Radziwill, to do the work. Dissatisfied with the result she had asked the New York decorator

Elisabeth Draper for advice before turning to Sister.[3] All in all it was an awkward situation, which might have been taken as a forewarning of things to come. Jack Kennedy initially baulked at any further redecoration but later relented and agreed to the work. He was by then on the campaign trail and perhaps this was a way of keeping Jackie occupied and amused. It appears that extensive work was undertaken, but regrettably there seem to be no photographs of the interiors Sister created. However, many of the furnishings were later reused in the White House and at Glen Ora, the house the Kennedys leased as a country retreat.

Glen Ora belonged to Mrs Gladys Tartiere.[4] Lying two miles south-east of Middleburg in Fauquier County, a convenient distance from Washington, Glen Ora was a large nineteenth-century house, built on the site of a smaller earlier house. The property was once part of a large parcel of land owned by Lord Fairfax, which was surveyed in 1747 by the sixteen-year-old George Washington.[5] In about 1800 the proprietor of what is today the Red Fox Tavern in Middleburg, a gentleman with the wonderful name of Noble Beveridge, bought a small tract of land and built a house at the 'mouth of a glen', hence the name. Noble Beveridge died in 1844, leaving Glen Ora to his niece Elizabeth Noland (the great-great-grandmother of the Charlotte Noland who founded Foxcroft School). Glen Ora eventually passed to the Tabb family and it was the last of the Tabbs who sold the property to Mr and Mrs Raymond Tartiere in 1938. At this time the house was no longer lived in, nor were the farms worked. With the help of the architect Henri de Heller the Tartieres set about restoring and reconfiguring the house to accommodate the collection of French furniture and pictures they brought from their houses in Paris and at Fontainebleau.

When Mrs Tartiere rented the house to President and Mrs Kennedy in 1961 she probably didn't appreciate all the implications (though she did remark, apropos the hard bargain driven by Jack Kennedy, that she felt the nation's finances would be in safe hands).[6] The house was rented furnished, but as the Kennedys brought their own furniture most of Mrs Tartiere's furniture ended up in the White House warehouse. Of course, secure telephone lines needed to be installed, room found for Secret Service personnel, police posts built, and gates added to the drive for security. On top of all this, needless to say, even though it was to be only a short tenancy, Jackie wanted changes. As Sister acknowledged, Jackie had a 'love of houses and [with] her feelings for colour and comfort, could not be content with things as they were'.[7] However, apart from the addition of an extra dressing room and bathroom, most of the work inside the house was pure decoration.

In the sitting room a new beige rug was laid, new chintz curtains were hung and slipcovers were made in the same chintz for the sofas. Mrs Tartiere's Louis XVI chairs were given new slipcovers in coral linen edged in red, which was also used for cushions for the sofa, so the colour was carried round the room. The dining room had a white rug from the Georgetown house and new curtains of yellow linen trimmed with a yellow and white fringe, but otherwise Mrs Tartiere's furniture seems to have been retained. Jackie particularly liked a mural by Nicholas de Moles depicting Mrs Tartiere's favourite parts of Paris.

The bedrooms were all repapered and/or repainted. Jackie's bedroom, with its adjoining bathroom, was papered in a 'pink, green and white paper', probably a floral print. A new white rug was used and the curtains were made, and the bed headboard covered, in a fabric that matched the wallpaper. Two dust flounces were in the same fabric, but plain white chintz, 'all piped in green chintz', was used as a backdrop. The surviving notes say the 'bed canopy, and one chair and ottoman in same chintz' – presumably white chintz. There was another armchair in quilted white fabric, and there were white tambour curtains in the dressing room.[8]

The President's bedroom seems to have been a recreation of his room in Georgetown. In came his sleigh bed with its special bed board and mattress, while the walls were painted white, and the same red carpet was used together with the same red and white toile curtains.

When Mrs Tartere got her house back she retained very little of Sister's work. For example, although she kept the pink, white and green floral paper in the dressing room, she felt it was too dominant in her bedroom, which she had painted a shade of blue.

However, as Glen Ora was a private residence, its decoration was a relatively straightforward job. The security expenses were of course met by the public purse, but President Kennedy picked up most of the bills personally. All the redecoration did add up – eventually to $10,000. The President 'raised hell', but he had no choice but to pay up.[9]

Of course, things were not quite so simple at the White House. Soon after Kennedy's election victory Jackie telephoned Mamie Eisenhower to arrange to be shown around. At first Jackie hatched the harebrained idea that Sister could tag along as her 'secretary', but Sister pointed out that this would be inappropriate and potentially deeply embarrassing. So Jackie went alone, at noon on 9 December, arriving in her dark blue station wagon driven by a Secret Service agent. James West, the Chief Usher, recalled that 'dressed in a dark blue coat, wearing hat and gloves, she could have been a young Congressman's wife paying an obligatory call.' James West introduced himself and escorted her to the Diplomatic Reception Room on the ground floor before they took the elevator up to the second floor where Mrs Eisenhower stood ready to greet her. Mr West withdrew. At exactly 1.30 p.m., 'two buzzers rang, indicating First Lady descending, and I dashed to the elevator.' They all walked out of the south entrance, said goodbye and 'Mrs Eisenhower stepped regally into the back seat of her Chrysler limousine and disappeared, off to her card game.'[10]

James West, Chief Usher at the White House throughout the Kennedy presidency.

Jackie was dismayed by what she found that December afternoon. The White House at that time was in a rather sorry state. When President Truman succeeded Franklin D. Roosevelt in April 1945 the building was found to be structurally unsafe, many of the roof timbers having rotted. The whole house was gutted, with only the outer walls remaining. The rooms were reassembled and redecorated, but not with any particular flair or conviction, nor much historical understanding. Over its history the interior of the house had been altered and reconfigured, the most extensive remodelling being carried out in 1902 by the New York architects McKim, Mead and White, who adopted the Beaux Arts style.

Jackie was not alone in wanting to bring some order and style to the White House. Grace Coolidge, wife of President Calvin Coolidge, who held office from 1923 to 1929, had made a valiant attempt, but her efforts were hampered by controversies over whether the building should be restored to its original state or later developments, particularly the Beaux Arts work, should be retained.

Astonishingly, the White House was not a protected building, but was subject to the whims of succeeding presidents and first ladies. Presidents could also remove items from the house upon leaving office. When President Truman left he took two chimneypieces with him from the East Room. The Kennedy administration were surprised to discover that no one legally 'owned' the White House. Proposals were drafted by the Deputy Attorney General which resulted in the White House being declared, by a 1961 Act of Congress, a museum and a part of the National Parks Service.[11] This protected not only the fabric of the building, but also its contents.

From the day of her first visit the restoration of the White House was Jackie's major project. Soon after she became First Lady she convened a committee for the restoration, to be known as the Fine Arts Committee or, as she nicknamed it, 'my Politburo'. This was formed under the chairmanship of Henry du Pont, owner of Winterthur in Delaware and a great authority on American furniture and decoration. Other influential members of the committee were Mrs Charles Engelhard, Mrs Douglas Dillon, John Loeb, Mrs Paul Mellon and Jackie's close friend Jayne Wrightsman.[12] Following the passage of the White House Act the Fine Arts Committee was able to solicit gifts and donations, assuring the donors that their gifts were inalienable. It was decided that lists should be drawn up of items required for various rooms. The procedure to be followed when a gift was offered was described as follows: 'A picture should be taken of the article and sent, together with at least one recognized expert's opinion of its authenticity, to Mrs Parish at the New York office, 22 East 69th Street. If a gift is not acceptable, Mr Finley, of the Fine Arts Commission, will refuse it in the name of our Committee, so as not to offend any friends.'[13] It is interesting that at this stage it was Sister Parish, rather than Henry du Pont, who was put in charge of the selection of suitable objects.

However, Jackie almost immediately involved in the redecoration not only Sister but also Stéphane Boudin, though White House officials went to some pains to conceal the extent of Boudin's involvement. It was not thought appropriate, and must certainly have appeared politically ill advised, to have a French designer in charge of the decoration of the White House.

But on 21 January 1961, the day after President Kennedy's inauguration and the Kennedys' first full day in the White House, it was just Jackie and Sister. The immediate priority was to sort out the private rooms, a suite of seven rooms on the second floor where the family was going to live. On her first visit Jackie had discovered that these rooms were 'neglected and lacklustre, furnished with department-store furniture and cheap hotel-style objects'.[14] Worse, there was no kitchen or dining room. Something had to be done, and quickly.

Jackie originally wanted her children in rooms opposite her own across the west hall on the north-west corner of the mansion, but as the servants' elevator was in that area it was decided to place the kitchen and dining room there. What had been President Eisenhower's mother-in-law's room – all done out in 'Mamie pink' – became the new family kitchen, while Mrs Truman's music room became the dining room.[15] Mr West, in consultation with René Verdon, the Kennedys' French chef, ordered a stainless steel and white kitchen with commercial-size ovens and refrigerators.

Initially the dining room was simply painted, but in late 1961 the walls were hung with 'Scenes of the American Revolution', a later version of the 'Scenic America' wallpaper used in the Diplomatic Reception Room on the ground floor. This paper, by the French manufacturers Zuber, was acquired and its installation paid for by Sister's friend and client Brooke Astor. It was a generous gift. Similarly, much of the fine American Federal furniture was bought by Mr and Mrs Charles Engelhard. This included a harlequin set of New York Sheraton-style dining chairs used with a triple pillar dining table of similar date. For the two windows Sister, in consultation with Henry du Pont and his pattern books at Winterthur, designed asymmetrical treatments in blue silk, trimmed with a green tassel fringing. A deeper tone of silk was used for the valances and jabots. It was perhaps a rather over-elaborate arrangement.[16]

The new dining room was a great success, but it was overshadowed by the room that served as the main sitting room. Although in the private apartments, the room could be termed a 'semi-state' room, as it was, and still is, used by the President and First Lady for entertaining. Above the Blue Room in the State Apartments, it is also oval in shape, running round the semicircular south portico, with magnificent views to the Washington Monument in the Mall. Sister decided to decorate the room in yellow. In doing so she was following historical precedent. In the early nineteenth

century, during President Madison's time, the room had
'furniture upholstered in yellow damask and curtains – with
festoons and fringes – made of the same material'.[17] Sister
may also have been influenced by Nancy Lancaster's famous
Yellow Room (see page 59). The tone of yellow Sister chose
was considerably paler than the one Nancy used, and dado
panelling and other woodwork were painted off-white.

Sister arranged for the decoration of this room to be
paid for by John and Frances Loeb, who were old friends.[18]
So it was the Loebs who picked up the $8,155.94 bill for
the yellow silk curtains with their bobble fringing and wide
patterned border. The design of these curtains and attendant
drapes appears to have been a joint endeavour between
Sister and Stéphane Boudin.[19] By most accounts the original
design was Boudin's, though, in consultation with Henry du
Pont, Sister adapted it to hang the curtains within the window
architraves (both Boudin and Jayne Wrightsman favoured
installing the curtains outside the mouldings, which would
have slightly increased the window exposure). However,
Albert Hadley – who had by then joined Sister as a partner –
claimed that the curtain sketch designs were Parish-Hadley
designs. To unify the room Sister used a yellow oval rug
formed from cut pile (probably a twist pile) carpeting that
was edged with an off-white fringe to give the appearance
of a rug rather than a carpet. Initially Sister used chairs and
sofas, including a set of Louis XVI style chairs, that had been
brought from the Kennedys' Georgetown house, together
with some pieces taken from the White House collection.
Then in June of 1961 Jayne Wrightsman – or, more likely,
Boudin – found in Paris a large suite of Louis XVI furniture by
Jean-Baptiste Lelarge. The *canapé*, six armchairs and six side
chairs were bought for $15,000 and repainted by Jansen.[19]
This suite replaced the Kennedys' furniture. The room was
unmistakably American, but it had that 'dash of French', as
John Fowler would say. One of his disciples, Keith Irvine,
described the room as having 'an American purity about it,

RIGHT AND OPPOSITE The First Lady's
bedroom. It was originally intended
that the walls should be pale green, as
in Jackie's bedroom in the Kennedys'
Georgetown house, but Jackie
ultimately decided on off-white,
which unbalanced the scheme.

with this lovely light-hearted French injection . . . all done
with a palette that was so sunshiny'.[20]

The President's and the First Lady's bedrooms also
looked out across the Mall. The President's room (now used
as a private sitting room) was a rather odd shape. Probably
during the Truman era, the room had been truncated to
provide an internal bathroom and a closet/dressing room
with access to the First Lady's room beyond. This meant
the chimneypiece was off-centre and the whole room had
a lopsided appearance, which made it a difficult room to
furnish. From Sister's bag of fabric samples the President
chose a toile in blue and white with a pattern of angels
blowing trumpets. The fabric had been proposed for
Caroline's bedroom, but the President said he had 'always
loved angels', so it was used to dress his four-poster bed
and for the window curtains. Continuing the blue and white

theme Sister used an open weave in blue and white for
the sofa, while for his rocking chair and a wing chair she
used off-white sailcloth. The carpeting was also off-white.
Between the windows stood a Philadelphia tall chest (or
'highboy') which was among the finest pieces of furniture
donated to the restoration project.

The First Lady's bedroom lay beyond. Jackie
initially wanted 'our bedroom to be the same as it was in
Georgetown', but as the two houses were quite dissimilar
this was hardly possible. Sister's plan was to use the same
off-white carpet as in the President's room and to have all
the woodwork in off-white, but to paint the walls a pale
green, as in the Georgetown house. However, at some point
Jackie changed her mind and decided to have off-white
walls. This made the scheme appear rather anaemic and
bland. Sister also used the same fabric as in Georgetown

for the curtains. This was a simple cotton of white and green daisies on a water-green ground, which Jackie later described as a 'rather country-type material', adding, 'of course, they looked absurd as the proportions of the room were so formal.' Sister designed some attractive festoon and tail draperies which hung within the mouldings. The water-green background colour was picked up by the bed corona, in a water-green silk, with an upholstered headboard in the curtain fabric. A sofa stood beside the fire with a large skirted table opposite, loaded with family photographs. Around the room stood Louis XV and XVI chairs, some upholstered in white damask, some in green silk, and others in gold-on-ivory cut velvet.

Next door, on the south-west corner, was the First Lady's dressing room and bathroom. Of all the rooms in the private apartments this was the one most altered by Boudin, to such an extent that most traces of Sister's work were removed. Sister's room had been quite simple, complementing the bedroom, but all traces of this 'casual Southampton vocabulary' were swept away.

The children were allocated rooms off the central hall, overlooking the north entrance. Caroline had the larger room. Sister painted the walls off-white and used the same off-white carpet as in the President's and First Lady's bedrooms. The wooden furniture was all painted white. A diminutive American Colonial four-poster bed was dressed with a small rosebud chintz with a spot ground, with the bed curtains lined in pink silk, which was also used to edge the curtains. A small sofa had loose covers of a pinky/red 'dot and cross' chintz, a fabric much used by John Fowler (though this example was probably a commercial fabric and not an exclusive from Colefax and Fowler).

ABOVE The President's bedroom. The Philadelphia highboy was among the finest pieces of furniture donated to the restoration of the White House.

LEFT The colour board prepared in Sister's office for the President's bedroom.

RIGHT President Kennedy himself chose the blue and white toile with a pattern of angels that was used to dress the four-poster bed and for the window curtains.

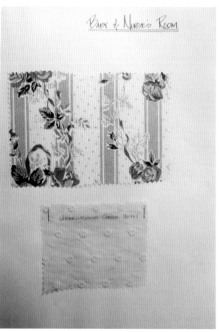

FAR LEFT The colour board prepared by Sister's office for Caroline Kennedy's bedroom.

LEFT The colour board for John Junior's bedroom.

BELOW The West Hall, which was used as the family sitting room.

OPPOSITE ABOVE John's room.

OPPOSITE BELOW Caroline's room.

John's room also had off-white walls and carpet with a blue-grounded chintz used for the curtains and loose covers. His cot was dressed in white muslin edged with lace. Again all the furniture was painted white, with the exception of a child's version of his father's famous rocking chair.[21]

All the work on the private apartments was completed in just six weeks. Mind you, Jackie and Sister managed to spend on these rooms alone the entire redecoration grant of $50,000 allocated by Congress to each new administration. As the exterior had also been 'dressed in its four-yearly coat of white paint the previous summer, there was absolutely no money left to put grandeur into the state rooms'.[22] Ever resourceful, Jackie suggested financing the work on the State Apartments not only through donations, sponsorship and gifts, but also by using the profits from the sale of guidebooks. Moreover,

following an interview Jackie gave to CBS she received a useful cheque for $10,000 towards the restoration.

Of the State Apartments on the main floor the only one Sister decorated was the Family Dining Room, where she worked closely with Henry du Pont. The decoration of this room was sponsored by Sister's clients Mr and Mrs Charles Engelhard, and by the time work began Albert Hadley had joined her as partner. The room had been redesigned in 1902 as part of the McKim, Mead and White alterations, and had been cast in a neoclassical vein. Robert Raley, the consulting architect at Winterthur, was brought in to modify and simplify the design. He removed the mouldings which had been added above the dado to form panels, but he retained the frieze. These modifications enhanced the room and did not detract from its most unusual feature, the vaulted ceiling.[23]

LEFT The cartoon for the carpet proposed for the Family Dining Room.

OPPOSITE The Family Dining Room arranged for the reception following President Kennedy's state funeral.

The ceiling was painted off-white, while the walls were done in a yellow that was similar in tone to that used in the Yellow Oval Room in the private apartments. The elaborate frieze was picked out in white on a yellow ground, and all the remaining mouldings were in white. Although Jansen's were not involved in the decoration of the room, the chimneypiece – green and white marble, featuring an eagle – was purchased through them. It had originally been intended for the Yellow Oval Room, but it was found to be far too small, as indeed it is even here. Jansen's also made proposals for the curtains, but Albert Hadley had already created two different schemes,

and a pared-down and simplified version of one of these was used. The curtains were basically strung back, with tie-backs lower down, and hung, as elsewhere, within the mouldings. Jackie was unenthusiastic about the whole room, describing it as 'her most unfavourite of all the White House rooms'.[24]

The other principal state rooms, the Red Drawing Room, the Green Drawing Room, the Blue Room, the State Dining Room and the East Room, were mostly decorated by Boudin, though Sister was involved to a small extent in some of the rooms (and, at an early stage, rearranged the furniture in all of them). Henry du Pont wanted the Red Room

decorated with furniture by Duncan Phyfe,[25] but eventually it was decided that it should be in the French Empire style. A number of Empire period textiles were sourced by Boudin and Sister approached Bergamo in New York about their reproduction. However, in the end another New York textile company, Scalamandré, reproduced the fabrics, perfectly.

The Green Room, the companion to the Red Room, was furnished with late eighteenth-century furniture in the Federal style. This furniture, much of which had been assembled by Grace Coolidge in 1928, set the scene and it was to remain a Federal-style parlour. Boudin detested it – 'the proportion is all wrong . . . these should not be so dainty', or, more succinctly, 'It is full of legs !'[26] The walls were to be hung with green silk moiré reproduced from a late eighteenth-century moss-coloured silk selected by Boudin. What appealed to Jackie was the variation in the pattern, which could only be reproduced if the fabric was woven by hand. Scalamandré sent a machine-woven sample of almost identical shade but lacking the character of the original. In the end Boudin engaged Tassinari and Châtel of Paris to weave the fabric, but the White House never admitted that a French company rather than Scalamandré had done the work.[27]

ABOVE The Green Drawing Room with the furniture arranged by Sister, shortly after it was redecorated.

RIGHT The Red Drawing Room, decorated in the French Empire style.

Boudin noticed everything and wanted to change most things. In the Blue Room a round table cloth in gold silk damask, with tassel trimmings in the same colour done by Sister, was deemed to look 'like a fat Spanish dancer'.[28] It had to go. The redecoration of the Blue Room was planned around a suite of furniture made by the Parisian cabinetmaker Pierre-Antoine Bellangé in 1817 for President Monroe, although by 1961 very little of the suite remained. A pier table was found and restored, and after this appeared in the press a chair from the same suite was donated by a member of the public. Eventually four chairs from the original suite returned once more to their original home. Controversially the room was hung with a cream-on-cream silk stripe with a continuous valance of light blue silk taffeta. Jackie was delighted with the result, the President less so – he felt the Blue Room should be blue – and Henry du Pont felt it was far 'too French'.[29] The room was completely redecorated in 1972, although the walls remain an off-white colour.

The most famous room in the White House is, of course, the Oval Office, from which the President runs his administration. On his first full day as president JFK found the Oval Office invaded by Jackie and Sister, who busied themselves moving the furniture. Sister's scheme for the room was relatively simple. She retained the green carpet and curtains that had been installed in 1947 for President Truman and contented herself with painting the walls off-white.[30] The President chose as his desk the famous desk carved from the timbers of HMS *Resolute* that had been presented to President Rutherford Hayes by Queen Victoria in 1880.[31] Continuing the nautical theme, Jackie borrowed a seascape of a battle during the 1812 war, to which she added other sea pictures and models of ships that the President had collected. The *Resolute* desk was placed in the accustomed position near the windows. Opposite, flanking the fireplace, Sister placed two large curved sofas with slipcovers in an oatmeal-coloured fabric, which was also used to cover a cushion for the President's rocking chair.

The room remained like this until 1963, when a redesign of the room by Boudin was mooted. Perhaps the impetus for the redecoration was Jackie's, but the President also seems to have been enthusiastic. The walls were painted a purer white and the green carpet from the Truman era was replaced by one of a deep wine red – the President liked red. New curtains in a pure white rep, edged by a red and gold braid, were ordered by Boudin and made up in France. The work was done in November 1963 when the President and First Lady were in Texas. President Kennedy never saw the completed room.

Henry du Pont strongly disapproved of Boudin's appointment. He felt that while Boudin was a great French decorator he was not qualified to decorate the American White House, and the end results were inevitably too French and did not live happily in the building. James Fosburgh, director of the Special Committee for White House Paintings, entirely agreed. He wrote to Jackie after his first meeting with Boudin to point out that 'he knows nothing about American painting or, for that matter, American furniture' and went on to say that there was little point in his acquiring things for the house since there was 'no reason to suppose that it will not be discarded or relegated to the attic as soon as he [Boudin] sees it'.[32] He had a point. Some of Boudin's work was far too theatrical for its context. It is interesting to compare his work at the White House with John Fowler's at Buckingham Palace, where Fowler decorated the Queen's Audience Room at about the same time. Fowler's work perfectly captured the mood of the room and its function. It remains unchanged, whereas all Boudin's work in the White House has been swept away (it lasted barely ten years) for more historically accurate work, which is what Henry du Pont wanted all along.

The Oval Office from behind the
Resolute desk. President Kennedy's
rocking chair stands between the
oatmeal sofas.

Looking the other way, towards the
desk and the windows. The curtains
date from the Truman restoration.
Their replacements were hung while
the President was in Texas. He never
saw them and they were immediately
removed.

The friendship between Jacqueline Kennedy and Sister did not survive the restoration of the White House. Various reasons have been advanced for why the friendship soured – from Sister's rebuking Caroline for putting her feet on the furniture to a misunderstanding over money (Jackie thought something didn't need to be paid for when it actually did). The most likely explanation might be that Jackie simply wanted to be rid of Sister so the whole project could be placed under the complete control of Boudin. She had no further need for Sister's services. Though undoubtedly hurt, for many years all Sister would say was, 'Jackie always got along better with men,' or 'Well, Jackie was very young.' Much later, in an unguarded moment, she was more forthright: 'The President was always a perfect gentleman,' she remarked, but 'Mrs Onassis [as Jackie was by then] was hell to deal with. Selfish, pretentious, cold, calculating – her taste was nil. The words "thank you" didn't exist in her limited vocabulary.' She added, for good measure, 'I'm sure she's a wonderful mother. But to me, she's a colorless cream puff.'[33] Nevertheless, Sister was always very proud of her work at the White House and some of the ideas she introduced still endure, most notably in the private apartments and the Yellow Oval Room.

In January 1961, while she was busy working on the White House, Sister's elder brother Frankie died very suddenly. He was just fifty-three. It was a hard blow. Sister was also becoming increasingly concerned about Harry's poor health (he had emphysema and asthma). Sitting one evening next to Van Day Truex at dinner, she told him that unless she could find a young person to help her she was going to close her business and retire. Van Day Truex knew just the man: his name was Albert Hadley.

Jacqueline Kennedy and her children leave the White House following President Kennedy's funeral.

87

PARISH HADLEY

Sister and Albert Hadley outside their offices at 22 East 69th Street, New York.

PREVIOUS PAGES Parish-Hadley 'Apple' in yellow.

PARISH
HADLEY

The following morning Van Day Truex telephoned Albert Hadley and asked him if he knew Sister and who she was – he did – adding 'She is waiting for you to call her.' Albert telephoned and arranged to meet Sister at her apartment at East 79th Street on Wednesday on the stroke of five. She opened the door herself in stockinged feet (a slight surprise) and he was then promptly bitten on the ankle by Yummy, her ferocious Pekinese. As Albert recalled, 'I went to her apartment, and we started talking, and we never stopped.'[1]

In many ways Albert Hadley was the perfect partner for Sister. Albert was born in Springfield, Tennessee, in November 1920. The Hadleys were an old Tennessee family; his grandmother, Mathilda Wade Hadley, was a descendant of John Donelson, who was one of the original settlers of Nashville. The Hadleys had built one of the finest plantation houses in the state, Vaucluse at Hadley's Bend, so named after a wide horseshoe bend in the Cumberland River. Vaucluse abutted President Andrew Jackson's estate, The Hermitage, and the two families were close friends.[2]

Albert never saw Vaucluse, but he had clear recollections of his mother's family house, Broadmoor. The house had grown in a rather haphazard manner, so it was not architecturally a consistent composition. Albert remembered the parlour, with its black marble chimneypiece and tall gilt overmantel mirror, the gilding reflected by the cornices. The gold theme continued with a 'heavy paper whose gold embossing outlined an all-over floral design in cream, tan, brown, and mossy green'. Moss-green brocatelle with a gold thread was used for the curtains and also as upholstery on some elaborate Victorian parlour furniture, which had belonged to Albert's great-grandparents. With its heavy lace undercurtains, upright piano and glass-shaded lamp set upon a marble-topped centre table, the room was a veritable pillar of Victorian respectability. Though he might not have been entirely sympathetic with the style and taste of the decoration, nevertheless, Albert said, 'I've never forgotten the allure of that room.'[3]

Albert's father, Albert Livingston Hadley, had a buggy and farm implements business in Springfield, but he sold this soon after Albert was born, and moved the family to Nashville. He bought a 'bright, boxy new bungalow in the fast developing outskirts of Nashville'.[4] Albert's first decorative endeavour, at the age of about three,

BELOW Albert Hadley, who joined
Sister to form Parish-Hadley in 1962,
and carried on the firm after she died.

BOTTOM Van Day Truex, a friend of
both Sister and Albert Hadley, and
the man who introduced them to
each other.

was to fill every hole in the caned footboard of his parents'
new ivory-painted bedroom suite. The bright blue indelible
pencil must have made quite a mess. Blue has remained one
of his favourite colours. The family soon moved again, to a
house built of cast cement, supposedly made to resemble
rusticated stone. Albert thought the house very ugly. In
1929 his father was offered a job by a big farm machinery
company, so the family moved yet again. His mother drew
up plans for her dream house based on ideas culled from
the pages of magazines. Built of yellow glazed bricks, it had
a shingle roof and dark green shutters, offset by white trim.
The interior was plastered out by a gang of Italian workmen
– *stuccadores* – who had unexpected and often undesired
flashes of artistic enthusiasm. They plastered the bedroom
walls with a plaster/sand mix to give a textured surface not
dissimilar in effect to Artex, the popular textured finish that
was much used in the 1960s and 1970s. Downstairs Mrs
Hadley managed to keep a tighter grip on the enterprising
Italians, explaining that what she wanted on her walls was
smooth plaster painted a creamy mustard ragged with soft
green, to give the room a translucent shimmering colour.
Albert was 'enthralled'. His mother would also go 'antiquing',
calling unannounced at farms and cottages asking if they had
anything they might wish to sell; many did.

Of course, Albert was addicted to *Vogue* and *House &
Garden* magazines. As a teenager he got a Saturday job at
Bradford's, Nashville's leading furniture shop. In 1941 he went
to work for A. Herbert Rodgers, one of the finest decorating
firms in the southern United States. Herbert Rogers was much
respected for his extensive architectural knowledge and his
understanding of French decoration and furniture. But he was
also a thoroughly practical man, and could do most of the
jobs he expected his workmen to do, firmly believing that a
good decorator understands how each task is accomplished.
As a junior assistant, Albert was exposed to all aspects of the
business. It was an excellent grounding.

The war disrupted everyone's life and Albert was drafted in 1942. He ended up in the 864th U.S. Division of Aviation Engineers where he was the company clerk (looking after the payroll). Arriving in the United Kingdom on 11 May 1942 – sailing into the Firth of Clyde – the division was promptly dispatched by train to London, and thence to Chelmsford in Essex. He could not have seen England at a lovelier time of year, though, as he recalled, 'all of the little villages that we passed through in this beautiful countryside were covered with waves of camouflage balloons'.[5] On his rare days off, like most of the soldiers on the camp, he would take the train up to London. Probably at the Rainbow Canteen in Piccadilly, where she was working, he met Lady Charles Cavendish, better known as Adele Astaire, Fred Astaire's sister. Through her he went on to meet Constance Spry, the celebrated florist, and subsequently Lady Mendl (Elsie de Wolfe). His military career was relatively brief for he was hospitalized with a chest infection in November 1943 and subsequently sent back to the United States. He was honourably discharged in January 1944.

In the summer of 1946 he went on holiday with a friend to Bridgeton in Maine. Returning from Maine he decided to stay on in New York, living at the YMCA on West 63rd Street. He wanted to be a decorator and decided to try and see every decorator he had read about in *House & Garden*, *Vogue* and *House Beautiful*. The man he most wanted to meet was William Pahlmann, who had formerly worked at Lord & Taylor. When they met, Pahlmann was charm itself and advised him to enrol at the Parsons School of Design, which is what he did.

He started his studies at the Parsons School of Design at 136 East 57th Street in June 1947 at the age of twenty-seven. The president of the school at this time was Van Day Truex. It was a three-year course, but by taking additional courses at the summer school, Albert managed to complete it in two years, graduating in June 1949. He soon got a job as

an assistant at Town and Country, a shop on Third Avenue and 50th Street owned by Roslyn Rosier, but he hardly had time to sharpen his pencils when Van Day Truex telephoned and asked him to join the teaching staff at Parsons, which he did in September 1949. He taught at Parsons for four years but when Van Day Truex left in early 1954 Albert resigned too, leaving in June. Soon after he started business on his own account, opening Albert Hadley, Inc., with a studio on East 57th Street. Life was tough, however: it was difficult to establish a decorating business without a retail outlet or a well-connected address book.

So in 1956 he went to work for Mrs Eleanor Brown at McMillen, one of the old-established decorating businesses (she had decorated Sister Parish's first married home in 1930). Albert became assistant to Ethel Smith, who was the senior decorator. As assistant it was Albert's responsibility to project manage the jobs, making sure things were done in the right order and correctly. One of the first jobs he did was a house in Hobe Sound, Florida, owned by Douglas Dillon (it was from Dillon's father that Sister rented her farmhouse in Far Hills). The Dillon house was 'bright, crisp and very up-to-date'.[6] He next worked for Mr and Mrs Milton Underwood, a wealthy Texan couple who had just bought Rosedown Plantation in St. Francisville, Louisiana. Albert persuaded the Underwoods to restore Rosedown, which, with McMillen's help, they did.

It was while working for McMillen, where he was the only male decorator, that he got his first piece of publicity. He was asked by *Vogue* to design a room, which was published in June 1959 under the title 'Fashions in Living: Summer on a Shoestring – Before and After' in *House & Garden*, *Vogue*'s sister magazine. He worked for McMillen's for five years, but in 1960, as he turned forty, he was becoming restless. Then in early 1961 Eleanor Brown gave the *New York Times* an interview in which she said that woman were always better decorators than men – she had never thought much of the

ABOVE LEFT Sister with Yummy, in her apartment at 39 East 79th Street.

RIGHT Sister and Albert Hadley in Moscow, where they decorated the American ambassador's residence.

OPPOSITE The hall of the Bronfman apartment, the first project Sister and Albert Hadley undertook together. It was a wonderful fusion of her traditional taste and his modernism.

work of William Pahlmann, Albert's hero, or of Billy Baldwin, a good friend. He resigned.

As soon as the formal details had been worked out, Albert telephoned Van Day Truex to tell him he was leaving McMillen's. Truex's phone call about Sister Parish came the following morning. Thus he found himself that October afternoon being savaged by Yummy. A deal was struck: Albert was to start at Mrs Henry Parish II Interiors on Tuesday 2 January 1962. She telephoned him the day before, summoning him to look at an apartment at 740 Park Avenue she was to decorate for Edgar Bronfman, the chairman of Seagram.

Sister, who seldom altered what she found, initially saw the Bronfman apartment as a restoration job. However, it quickly became clear that the client had other ideas. Having merely run a tape measure round the place and taken a few notes, Sister received a telegram from Bronfman, who was in

Mexico, ordering that no further work be undertaken until his return, as he wanted a 'floating apartment'. Somewhat bewildered, Sister was forced to ask, 'What in God's name do they mean by a floating apartment?' Albert knew exactly what was wanted. He had come from a different tradition. At McMillen's anything was possible to achieve the desired result. Working with the architect Jack Cobel, he basically gutted the apartment and reconfigured it in a modern style. To achieve the look the Bronfmans wanted, the walls were stopped short, so the ceiling appeared to float beyond with no visible means of support. This created crisp modern spaces, which Sister proceeded to fill with antique French furniture of the highest quality, which took on a sculptural quality within the space. It was clever and somehow worked beautifully.

The Bronfman apartment was an important commission for it fused Albert's modernist instincts and Sister's traditional tendencies. The whole project was an amalgam of their

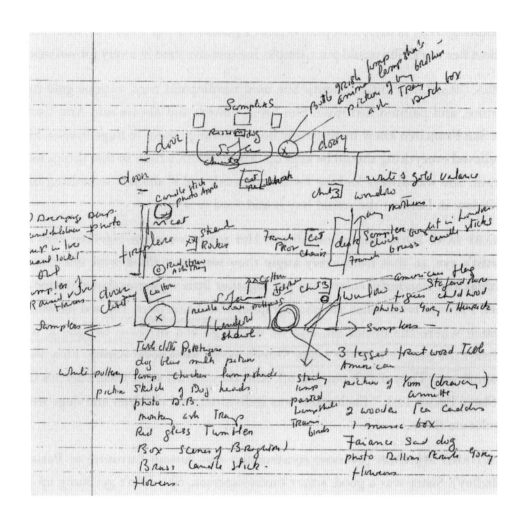

qualities, and this set a pattern for how they were to work for the next thirty years.

Sister's style was intuitive rather than studied. As Albert remarked, her sense was 'so magical, she couldn't often explain what she wanted'. She 'could just tell what a house needed' and the guiding philosophy was 'what the room wants', an oft-repeated phrase at Parish-Hadley.[7] It echoes John Fowler's dictum: 'You must do right by the house.'

At this stage of her life she produced no plans at all. All the design work was done in her head, where it remained. In later years she did do room plans, or more accurately sketches. They were basically doodles where every element was the same size, from a sofa to a table lamp. These doodles her staff would be expected to interpret. One assistant complained, 'Oh Mrs Parish, we scaled it in and it won't fit', only to be sharply told, 'Don't be ridiculous, of course it will fit,' which of course it always did.[8] Not that it really mattered for when she went to a job as it was being 'installed' she would change everything around, and it always looked far better for it. Sister would usually take the curtain-maker, the upholsterer and the painter to the job and explain what she wanted and how she wanted the room to look. The curtain-maker would measure, as would the upholsterer, and along with the painter they would all calculate. It worked.

When Albert joined Sister her firm was tiny – basically her, an assistant, a secretary and a bookkeeper. Most of her work was located along the East Coast, but in the mid-1950s she had undertaken a large commission in South Africa for the Englehards, friends and neighbours in New Jersey. As to comply with currency regulations everything required for the project had to be purchased within the sterling area, she asked John Fowler of if he would lend her one of his staff from Colefax and Fowler in London to run the job: he sent her Keith Irvine.[9] Later, Keith worked for Sister in New York as an assistant, staying for about nine months. They parted on bad terms and ignored one another for the next fifteen years.

Coming from Colefax and Fowler, where architecture was regarded as 'the bones of the business', Keith found Sister's lack of interest in the subject disconcerting. He did think she was very good at 'girls' bedrooms' – she had a knack of making them feminine and pretty – and he thought she had a particular talent for making beds look attractive and comfortable. In England four-poster beds (even John Fowler's) 'always look like there is a dead body in them'![10] Billy Baldwin went even further, telling Valentine Lawford that 'through all the years, Sister has done – and still does – by far the most attractive, seductive, luxurious bedrooms of any decorator in America.'[11]

Because in the early years she worked mostly for friends, or friends of friends, her business was organized in a very informal manner – she did not even prepare estimates. It was all basically done on trust. Working on the White House changed the nature of the business. Recognizing that it needed to be organized on more formal lines, Albert asked the bookkeeper at McMillen's to come and set up some systems. Henceforth estimates would be prepared and contracts issued, so everyone knew where they were. Sister soon began to appreciate Albert and to rely upon him. She even confided to the decorative painter Richard Lowell Neas (then working for the firm at Greentree, the Whitney estate on Long Island) that 'meeting Albert saved my life.'[12]

The year 1962 was full of exciting and interesting projects both at home and in the United Kingdom. Parish-Hadley did an apartment in London's Mayfair for Charles Englehard where the walls were painted in buttercup yellow with a high gloss finish, very similar to Nancy Lancaster's apartment just down the road. At home they did a house, Cove End in Northeast Harbor in Maine, for Brooke Astor.

Here Albert spent a huge amount of time meticulously working out every last detail, drawing scaled floor plans which were basically disregarded the moment the removal truck pulled into the drive. As Albert recalled, Sister 'wasn't intimidated by my approach, but she didn't understand it either.' On the other hand, watching sofas, chairs and tables fly in all directions, Albert saw and understood Sister's 'baroque, freewheeling style of working'. As he said, 'I was completely entranced.'[13] Her attitude and philosophy was: 'Forget the floor plans. Arrange the furniture where it is the most comfortable and will look best.'[14] She did have a knack for arranging furniture. It was always said that she could get more furniture into a room than any other decorator. As Mark Hampton – who worked at Parish-Hadley during the summer of 1963 and became a great favourite of Sister's – commented, 'Mrs Parish can do a medium-sized drawing room with thirty places to sit, no problem.'[15]

With Albert's arrival Sister's style began to evolve. As he remarked, 'If early in our collaboration Sis had heard of modernism, it didn't interest her very much, but I was the disciple.' Things that were to become hallmarks of the Parish-Hadley style, such as 'lacquered walls, modern lighting, even classic Oriental tables bound in raffia and dipped in enamel paint, were included in my design vocabulary.'[16]

They also decided to produce their own fabrics. Some were based on 'documents' (historical fabrics) but they were simplified or stylized and recoloured, usually in bright, vivid colours. In addition, they began to create custom pieces of furniture, lamps, carpets and rugs, and other accessories. The theme that linked all these products was the spirit of twentieth-century design.

ABOVE FAR LEFT A traditional arrangement of mantelpiece, candlesticks and mirror in the Bronfman apartment.

BELOW FAR LEFT The decorator Mark Hampton, who first worked for Sister in 1963, and became a great friend.

LEFT A typical example of a floor plan drawn up by Sister, with a strong emphasis on the placing of objects, and everything drawn much the same size.

RIGHT The Englehard apartment in Grosvenor Square, Mayfair. The work was carried out in conjunction with Colefax and Fowler, who usually worked on Sister's British projects.

Wallpapers produced for Parish-Hadley.
RROM LEFT TO RIGHT: 'Burmese', 'Apple', and 'Chou-Chou'.

CHOU-CHOU

They also encouraged others. It was Sister and Albert who encouraged Alan Campbell to start his fabric business. He had heard of Sister long before he actually met her, as he shared a summer cottage on Fire Island with a group of friends, including Kevin McNamara, who worked at Parish-Hadley. She seemed to be a perennial topic of remarks, many of them derogatory! Naturally he was fascinated to meet this ogre, who was loathed and feared, but evidently also greatly loved. When he did meet her he was charmed. He began doing batik, and gave one item to Albert, who naturally showed it to Sister. He soon found himself bidden to dinner and she commissioned some cushions from him. In no time his work was published, he was making fabric for Halston, and half fashionable New York was wearing caftans made from his fabrics.

The decorating and style magazines, always eager for a story or a new angle, were soon busy writing about the firm, and Albert was adept at gaining publicity. While he was interested in modernism, Sister was fascinated by crafts and folk art. According to Nancy Novogrod, a former editor of *House & Garden*, she was 'the first significant champion of using American crafts in decorating'.[17] She loved painted floors, rag rugs, wickerwork, painted valances, hand-woven bedspreads, knitted throws and, of course, patchwork quilts.

Sister and Albert were introduced to the 'Freedom Quilting Bee' movement by Diana Vreeland, the editor of *Vogue*. This movement was founded in Rehoboth, Alabama, in 1966 by an Episcopalian minister, the Reverend Francis X. Walter. It was born out of the Civil Rights movement and was intended as a means whereby poor southern women (usually African-Americans) could earn some income. As Sister remarked, 'The largest number of workers is in Alabama. They are cotton pickers who do their sewing at night and sometimes make the patches from burlap sacks.'[18] Diana Vreeland sent the Reverend Walter round to Parish-Hadley's offices. Sister didn't like his fabrics, or their colours, and so Parish-Hadley sent him fabrics in the colours (all bright and vivid) she liked. The rest is history.

A corner of Sister's drawing room at 960 Fifth Avenue. The chair is covered in a fabric printed by Alan Campbell.

ABOVE A painted floor created by Parish-Hadley at a house in Maine. The design was adapted from an inlaid marble floor Sister had seen in England. The technique is interesting. First the floor is sanded and then the design is drawn out and inscribed with a knife, making a hairline cut that helps to keep the colours separate and prevent them from overlapping. Several coats of paint are applied and finally the floor is sealed with varnish.

TOP LEFT A bedroom in Maine with a painted floor.

TOP RIGHT In the Sister Parish Shop in Maine – quilts, rag rugs and a needlepoint rooster at the foot of the bed.

CENTRE LEFT White-painted wicker and rattan were always part of the Parish-Hadley style.

CENTRE RIGHT A kitchen enlivened with stencilling.

BOTTOM LEFT A blue-painted library with a large tiger-striped sofa.

BOTTOM RIGHT A small breakfast room with an unusual painted floor.

No one could have imagined how the look would take off, but it fitted into a trend. A London decorator recalled: 'I knew an antique dealer in Portobello Road who sold small pieces of French country furniture, which were invariably painted. I was drawn to them. Also I have always loved old needlework samplers and collected these. Quilts were a natural progression.'[19] At about the same time Laura Ashley was developing her fashion and home furnishings empire. Even in the early 1950s, when the Ashleys began printing textiles, Laura was drawn to small flower motifs, but these were impractical for their machinery. The huge expansion in their business came in the 1970s and was very much of its time. The Whitney Museum of American Art held an exhibition in 1971 of quilts collected by Jonathan Holstein and his wife, Gail van der Hoof. It was a huge success and led, three years later, to another exhibition, 'The Flowering of American Folk Art'.

Parish-Hadley went on to upholster a large sofa in quilted fabric for Bill and Babe Paley, for whom Parish-Hadley worked on a number of properties, and they used a quilted fabric for the dining room curtains at Senator Charles Percy's Washington home. In the 1960s Sister's bright, almost garish colours were the height of fashion. Her colour sense was highly developed. In much the same way as Nancy Lancaster had used strong colours for houses, such as Kelmarsh, which were in effect under-furnished, so Sister used colour, lots of pattern, and yet more colour, to make up for the lack of fine furniture and antiques.

Albert was soon indispensable to Sister and she quickly decided to make him a partner. The lawyers and accountants pored over the books and drew up an agreement. At the meeting they went over all the legal jargon, which neither Sister nor Albert understood, and neither was much interested in, although Albert noticed that Sister had been scribbling on her notepad throughout. After the meeting broke up Albert tided the room and discovered that Sister had actually been sitting doodling: her notepad was covered in dollar signs.[20] She knew this would be a hugely successful partnership, and so it turned out to be.

Commissions quickly rolled in. Soon they had far more work than either had expected, so they began to recruit assistants. Many well-known decorators of today began their careers at Parish-Hadley and it almost became a finishing school for decorators. Mark Hampton was an early member of staff, and Bunny Williams joined in 1967 and remained for the next twenty-two years. It was always Albert's policy to develop talent. As their confidence grew, the assistants would begin to bring in their own clients, and Albert would act as a sort of editor, reviewing their proposals and suggesting

LEFT In the Greek home of a London designer, folk art predominates. The large eathenware bowl is Greek, while the tole lantern is probably Portuguese. The chairs are those typically found in Greek tavernas.

ABOVE A quilted fabric used to make sofa covers, in 1968. This was an unusual choice, but characteristic of the innovative and quirky Parish-Hadley style.

improvements and alterations. Sister was not involved in these projects, although she knew about them.

When David Kleinberg went to work for Parish-Hadley in 1981 he thought – erroneously as it turned out – that he would be working for Albert. Sister had other ideas. David was interviewed by them both and remains convinced that he got the job because he mopped up after one of the Pekinese who peed on the carpet! Sister liked that, and he soon became her 'slave' of choice. He recalled 'we were all a bit intimidated by Sister', but she 'was always fair – could be judgmental – but always fair'.

Sister was very involved in jobs and would review everything. They would start to assemble a scheme around the principal fabric. As the assistant, you soon learnt what she would like and what she would not. For example, 'you could never bring Mrs Parish a chintz with birds – birds were bad luck.' She hated yellow bedrooms, so that was another no-no. She would feel the texture of any fabric sample brought to her, and would sometimes respond that it was too rough, or the colour too sharp. Her style was intuitive. Eventually the scheme, be it for a single room or a whole house, would come together. Only when it had her approval would it be presented to the client.

Sister loved to go shopping for furniture and she did have a wonderful eye – perhaps inherited from her father, who was a respected collector of eighteenth-century English furniture. She also loved to search for antique rugs; the patterns and colours were always a huge draw. She was less interested in the intricacy of curtain designs, continuing to rely on the stock patterns – she probably had about ten – that she had devised in the early years of her work. Albert recalled how, soon after he went to work with her, they were discussing how to treat a library window when Sister remarked, 'Number seven will do perfectly.' When asked what she meant, 'she pulled out of her bag a piece of cardboard with a handful of curtain designs on it, indicating the one she felt fit the bill.' Sister couldn't quite understand why McMillen's had no stock designs, and was surprised, and not a little shocked, to discover that Albert would have designs mocked up in muslin, and that they even paid 'good money to a young man who did nothing but scale lampshades'![21] But as things began to change Sister soon realized the worth of Albert's careful approach and his meticulously worked out designs and the value of having mock-ups done at the workroom to give an idea of the finished effect.

Of course, before getting to this point the client had to be accepted in the first place, and many who aspired were turned away. Sister and Albert always visited any new client together and as they knew one another so well Albert understood that 'Albert, I don't feel well; I must go home' actually meant, 'This is a waste of time, let's get out of here!' As Libby Cameron, who became an assistant in 1982, recalled, 'Hers was an emotional reaction to clients. She got involved with people's lives.'[22] Because she had personally selected her clients, Sister 'never walked away from anything she accepted. If she didn't like the client [or found she just couldn't get on with them] she would turn the job over to me,' Albert remembered. Clients almost invariably remained for years and it is hardly surprising that at least a quarter of the firm's work consisted of 'renewals', refreshing what had over the years become tired and worn. Of course, some clients would move house – 'downsizing', or in some cases 'upsizing' – and this too brought in a steady stream of work.

This was how the business grew and developed from that cold January day in 1962 when Albert joined her. When Sister died in September 1994 there were seven designers who shared three assistants, plus a small in-house architectural department. It was all a far cry from that tiny room in Far Hills rented for $35 a month sixty years before.

A Parish-Hadley group photograph.
FROM LEFT TO RIGHT: Brian McCarthy,
David McMahon, Sister, Albert Hadley,
Gary Hager, Libby Cameron,
David Kleinberg.

AN IDEA OF HOME

The Summer House, Dark Harbor, Maine. To Sister this was always home.

PREVIOUS PAGES Parish-Hadley 'Tucker' in seafoam.

AN IDEA
OF HOME

If home is where the heart is, in Sister's case home was Dark Harbor on the island of Isleboro in Maine. She may have lived most of her life in New York but it was in Maine that she was at her happiest and most relaxed. As Sister recalled, 'Dark Harbor is very special to me, and I owe a lot of what I am and what I do to that island.' She could, she said, 'smell the pines, feel the salt air, hear the waves lapping against the rocks. At night, wherever I am, I hear the seagulls calling, and sometimes in my dreams, it is so real I wake up and feel that I must go, be off to Dark Harbor, and right away.'[1]

The Kinnicutt family had long connections with Dark Harbor. Sorella, Sister's grandfather's house on the point, was mentioned in an article that appeared in *House & Garden* magazine in 1907. The description makes it sound wonderfully romantic: 'Situated close to the water's edge, with pine trees protecting it on three sides; red tile roof, white plastered walls, shuttered windows with heart-shaped openings, and white awnings make it an exact reproduction of a Devonshire cottage. Surrounded by a tiny strip of brilliant green lawn, and banked with flowers, it is quite ideal.'[2] Sister was not yet fifteen days old when she first visited Dark Harbor. Asleep in a white wicker bassinet bedecked with pink roses, she was carried aboard the Bar Harbor Express, which left Pennsylvania Station in New York in the early evening. At five in the morning the train pulled into Portland where it split in two. Eventually, around midday, the family arrived in Rockland, where a steamer met the train. On Isleboro the steamer was met by a collection of buggies and buckboards by which they made their way to Sorella.

After their marriage the Parishes were able to buy a small cottage on the same point in 1932 for $10,000, not an inconsiderable sum at the time. 'My father thought it was wickedly expensive,' Sister recalled.[3] Over the years Sister extended and adapted what was known as the Summer House and acquired other properties in the neighbourhood, including the Town House, a farmhouse painted a deep yellow, which was especially set up for use in the winter, and the Brown House, the Barn and the Red House, which were all essentially guest cottages. It became a veritable Parish village.

A decorator's own home is likely to be a far better reflection of their taste than anything done for a client, where what is being created is the stage for another's life, a reflection of their personality and interests. The Summer House was all Sister's. *House & Garden* magazine sent a photographer to the house in the summer of 1966. When the pictures arrived at their offices the editorial staff were stunned. They had never seen anything quite like it before. The house was published in *House & Garden* in January 1967 and it 'dazzled decorators the way Christian Dior's 1947 "New Look" did the fashion world. Along with the white furniture were deck painted floors, handmade cotton rugs, a mix or three or four softly coloured chintzes, paintings of dogs and all kinds of needlework.'[4] It caused a sensation. This is where 'American Country Style' began, or at least where it was first recognized.

Styles in decoration invariably have many strands and nuances. And so it is with American Style, which manifests itself in a number of permutations. There are three recognizable strands or sub-styles that are still in vogue even today. First, there is an Americanized version of the English Country House Style, so closely associated with Nancy Lancaster and John Fowler, and much admired by

Sister. She used this style in her work, but infused it with far more 'dashes of French' than any self-respecting Englishman would have countenanced. This American, Francophile version of the English style was much appreciated by the American East Coast rich who formed the majority of Sister's clients, and she often used it in their houses. Many other decorators also used this style, with varying degrees of success. Another strand is American Country Style, a strong, simple look which places much emphasis on American folk art. And there is yet another form, which is quaint and cluttered, a modern-day riot of Victoriana. The three versions have common elements and the boundaries are fluid and indistinct. There is no right or wrong way to do American Style; it is inclusive, not prescriptive.

Nowhere was American Style more deftly expressed than at the Summer House. The approach was modest and unassuming. A simple gravel drive, with notices warning of dogs and children (in that order), led down to a large turning circle, its centre planted with apple trees. A dark green wooden bridge with a large antique bell on one post passed over part of the pond towards the front door, set beneath its protective portico – grandeur on a diminutive scale. Neat beds nestled beneath the house walls and climbing roses festooned the trellises. From the tiny hall, turning left you found yourself in the parlour, a room that, in 1977, Sister said she hadn't 'touched for over forty years'.[5] There were some minor alterations – a wicker coffee table replaced one of white-painted wood, for example – but it is true that essentially the room remained unchanged. A hexagonal bay window looked out to the garden and ocean beyond and was dressed with Victorian-style curtains, complete with a deep frilled edge and tied back high almost like Italian stringing. The floral chintz was one of four used in the room, echoed in some loose covers, but contrasted with two other patterns used for upholstery and yet another for cushions. The unifying theme was the colour blue. The sofa was

upholstered in a blue chintz, the colour picked up by the other different but related, fabrics that were used, and the blue-striped rag rug laid upon the painted floor. The green paint colour reflected the foliage found in the chintzes.

It might seem that this riot of pattern would be heavy, busy and oppressive, and yet there was a tranquillity about the room. No one thing stood out and dominated, for she had mixed and combined so that she had movement everywhere. She had also used fabrics that had different scales and were

constructed on different pattern bases. The sofas and chairs were an odd assortment too, from a comfortable-looking camel-back sofa in the bay window to a Victorian drawing room sofa, stiff and formal in its propriety, and yet here, bedecked in a rose chintz, looking almost relaxed and at ease. There were pictures propped against the windows, while others – although in reality carefully placed against the striped wallpaper – looked as if they were casually hung from a rusty nail just knocked into the wall long ago by

BELOW LEFT The dining room as it was in the 1960s. The furniture, part of a set Sister bought in the 1930s for a dollar a piece, was originally polished oak. Sister had it all painted white.

BELOW RIGHT Around the parlour fireplace. The sofa, covered in a light chintz, is in the Victorian style.

some forgotten person. A white porcelain parrot on a swing, retired after many years of active service in New York, took careful note of the scene.

The room across the hall had originally been the dining room. This room was full of 'dollar a piece' furniture. After she had bought the Summer House, money probably a bit tight, Sister bought at a barn sale a hundred pieces of golden oak furniture for a dollar a piece – it was $100 well spent. She proceeded to have all of it painted in white enamel. The fat oak table legs, with their deep fluting, were given numerous coats, taking on an almost marble-like quality.

In the late 1960s some additional rooms were built. The dining room was moved to a new, more convenient location and the old room became the living room. The old dining table, covered with a chintz cloth, became a desk, set between two windows which appeared quite elaborately dressed, until you realized the curtains were a simple cotton and the valances were actually tin painted to resemble a yellow and white striped chintz with ribbon rosettes and tassels. A watermelon was in reality a piece of driftwood

Sister's daughter Apple painted, and the red colour of its wooden flesh was picked up by the comfortable armchair. The mantelpiece was decked with an embroidered valance of very fine quality pinned down by a pair of substantial-looking porcelain ducks and a large picture casually propped up, looking as if a decision was imminent on whether to hang it or not (or maybe to wait a few more years before finally deciding).

This led on in to the new dining room, which had sliding glass doors opening on to the garden. These patio doors might seem a rather surprising element in this traditional setting, but they worked well in the larger space. A new dining table was made for the room and given a marbled top edged with a *trompe l'oeil* ribbon design. The old straight-backed chairs from the previous dining room were reused and the same wool carpeting was run from the living room through into the new room. Although these new spaces were modern from an architectural point of view, they nevertheless harmonized with the rest of the house, a century and more their senior. The additions transformed

BELOW The new dining room, with large windows overlooking the garden.

RIGHT With chairs brought from the former dining room placed around a new painted table and the addition of folk elements – including a tin rooster – the room was an essay in American Country Style.

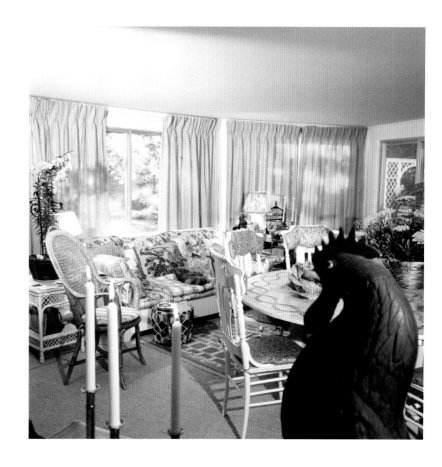

ABOVE The old dining room transformed into a living room. The valances are of tin painted to look like fabric, and the slice of watermelon is a piece of driftwood painted by Sister's daughter Apple.

LEFT Country style around the living room fireplace. Sister worked the teapot cushion herself. Pottery ducks sit on the mantelpiece, a pottery dog beside the armchair. And the rooster has found a new perch.

BELOW Sister's bedroom: eight
different patterns were used in
the room.

the house and provided a different entrance, which became a favourite. This back porch served as the breakfast room and also the laundry but was dominated by a huge birdcage with turrets and gables and topped by a dome. This was a typical example of the whimsical style that permeated much of the house.

There were two staircases. The narrow, treacherous-looking back stairs were given a painted runner with a *trompe l'oeil* cushion at the foot where a large marmalade cat slept soundly – or so one thought. The main staircase was equally narrow and awkward. Made by a former owner, one Captain Babidge, it might almost have been found on a ship. It rose straight up, reached a 3-foot-square landing step, turned 90 degrees, and rose again almost vertically. Here Sister had a real needlepoint runner she worked herself, and the rough, almost crude banister was balanced by a bamboo railing twined with foliage painted on the wall. Shelves with fruits, flowers and even a teapot were all charming examples of *trompe l'oeil*. An old French bread basket in retirement found a new purpose as an umbrella stand.

The layering of pattern evident in the reception rooms was even more pronounced in the bedrooms, resplendent with their four-poster beds. Sister's own bedroom was a good example. There were no less than eight different patterns, with flowers and colours in common. The wallpaper was a tiny white on pink floral pattern, strikingly similar to those produced by Laura Ashley in the late 1970s. The painted Regency bed, originally made for an army colonel, was simply dressed with plain white muslin edged by a fancy trim Sister acquired on a trip to Guatemala. A flowery old quilt covered the bed and lived happily with the rose chintz used for pillowcases. A different rose-patterned chintz, albeit in similar colours, was used for the curtains with their simple valance. Yet another chintz, this time with a blue ground, covered the ivory-coloured French fauteuil, and this was juxtaposed with a skirted bedside table with another pattern.

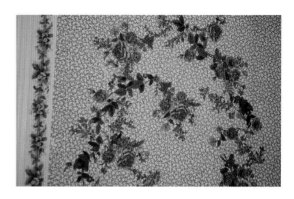

The dressing table was probably once a mahogany sideboard in a dining room, but a few coats of paint, and especially the addition of a fancy painted decoration, had altered its character so that it fitted perfectly here. A simple bleached chair, used for a dressing chair, with a seat pad of a blue and white print, toned down any hint of sophistication. Covering the floor was a rag rug in tones of pink.

The companion bed was in a guest room. Pushed into a corner of the small room, it was again hung with white muslin edged by a bobble fringe. In this room also, pattern was everywhere. A small spot pattern, again reminiscent of Laura Ashley but this time in the style of the late 1960s, covered the walls. The striped floral chintz covered the bed headboard and was also used, but at an angle, on a bedside table. A quilt of patterned hexagons covered the bed, while beside it there was a small flowery needlepoint rug.

The principal guest bedroom was much larger, and there was room for a big sofa, turning it effectively into a bedsitting room. Again the bed hangings, coverlet, window curtains and loose covers on the chairs and sofa were a medley of prints. In a corner was a small tent wardrobe covered in a small print, an idea copied from John Fowler in England. On the floor Sister spread Irish rugs in broad, bold stripes of colour hand-woven on narrow-width looms only 30 inches wide. Neither the stripes nor the colours themselves ever seemed to meet, but the anarchy was part of the charm. An old picnic basket set before the large sofa – a twin to that in the new dining room – became a coffee table, while a French screen hand painted with birds, which had once been in Harry Parish's bedroom in New York, blocked any view that might reasonably have been expected.

Sister always took breakfast in bed on a tray, as was the custom in English country houses. It was served at 7 a.m. (well, it was if the staff arrived on time). Later in the day she would sit on the porch, with its view to the southernmost tip of Seven Hundred Acre Island (where Nancy Lancaster would go to stay with her aunt Irene Gibson before the war) decorated with innumerable small yachts moored in the distance. There was a convenient telephone line, so she was able to chat to the office, giving her orders. At 6 p.m. she would have a bath, to re-emerge in 'pleated white silk shirt, narrow navy trousers with permanent creases, a heavy ribbed navy cardigan, white ballerina shoes, gold shell earrings, and a string of Barbara Bush pop beads'. She would

OPPOSITE FAR LEFT Sister chose to accentuate the idiosyncrasies of the upstairs bedroom, running a rose garland border around the eaves and across the ceiling. The miniature Victorian sofa, made for a furniture store as a display piece, was covered in a pink rosebud chintz.

OPPOSITE LEFT The guest bedsitting room was a medley of pattern and colour. The floor was strewn with striped carpet runners stitched together. The screen was brought up from New York.

BELOW The Town House sitting room in 1966. Patchwork, embroidered cushions and a large circular rug were mixed with chintz. The collection of samplers had belonged to Sister's mother.

enjoy a drink on the porch before supper, which might be chicken hash or salmon croquettes, followed by junket and apricot tapioca. Her 'house chowder' was made from local haddock with carrots and onions from her kitchen garden, and was served in green-glazed Provençal earthenware, with bamboo-handled cutlery.[6]

Much of her time was spent sitting on the porch, the deep padded bench seat strewn with gaily patterned and coloured cushions. It was always full of pots of flowers, almost bringing the garden into the house. Sister loved her garden, but she was not the sort of hands-on gardener that Nancy Lancaster was – certainly never one for what Nancy described as the real fun of gardening: getting 'flat down on your stomach and weeding with your teeth'. There were always masses of pots planted with jasmine, lilies, foxgloves, deep blue heliotrope and icy white petunias. In the trellis arches would be hanging baskets filled with pink begonias. As you gazed out from the porch the large silhouettes of firs and flashes of white from the branches and trunks of silver birches led the eye down to the water's edge. It was a charming place to sit and contemplate the world.

In Maine Sister was in family mode. Life was different from the bustle of New York, more relaxed and perhaps more friendly. Though basically a summer resident, she would also go there occasionally in the winter, staying at the Town House (although there was no town). The Town House was set up for winter with a good central heating system. *House & Garden* had the Summer House photographed again in 1970, this time along with the Town House, for an article which they published in March 1971. In this instance the photographs were taken by Horst P. Horst, probably the finest photographer of his generation.

The Town House was different from the Summer House in look and feel. The large greenhouse/conservatory opened into a small hall with a bright blue lacquer painted floor. Sister filled the hall with a curious collection of objects, including a gothic chair with ivory finials, masses of wicker baskets, a few birdcages and – carrying on the bird theme – a duck rug.

In the sitting room the first thing to catch the eye was a lampshade with an animal découpage that Sister had made herself; the next a large sofa covered with a pink and white geometric print designed by Albert Hadley.

OPPOSITE BELOW The Summer House
porch, where Sister spent much of
her time, and the view from the
porch out towards Seven Hundred
Acre Island far in the distance.

TOP RIGHT The Town House with its
large conservatory.

CENTRE RIGHT Sister taking tea on the
Summer House porch, with a crochet
rug to keep the chill at bay and
guarded by one of her ever-faithful
Pekinese.

BOTTOM RIGHT Sister and some young
friends on the flower-filled porch.

Old samplers, some of which had belonged to her mother, covered the walls, while masses of needlepoint cushions were piled on the sofa and old pieces of needlework carpeted the floor. The curtains were made from a rosebud chintz, and topped by quite sophisticated carved wood valances in white and gold. Sister's bedroom was even more of a mixture. There were no less than four different chintzes, but this was more by accident than design for, as she explained, 'I didn't do it intentionally or buy everything at once. When a chair needs covering, I do it.'[7]

The Brown House, which does not seem to have been published in any magazine, was a riot of colour – 'It was all sorts of rainbow colours: pale blue and shots of lavender and scarlet,' as Mark Hampton recalled. Beyond was the barn that Albert Hadley renovated and turned into his summer house. As you might expect Albert's house was radically different. It was done in a largely neutral palette, all beiges and whites. Sister hated beige, which she would describe as a 'terrible

kicky colour'. Albert's house was full of it. But it was also a house full of space, light and air.

One of Sister's 'favourite pastimes was snooping around other peoples houses'. At one point she had a pony called Kangaroo, who would pull her about the island in a wicker governess cart. Like her Pekinese, who seem to have been especially bred to be vicious (they all appeared to detest poor Albert Hadley), so Kangaroo was a mean-minded pony. During winter he stayed in Camden where he pulled Santa's sleigh, but because he hated children he would bite everyone in sight. As her daughter Apple remarked, Kangaroo 'was the type of animal Mummy liked – contrary. He had one green eye and one brown eye, and a mean glint in both of them.'[8] One day Sister decided to go 'snooping' at her brother Frankie's old house, which had been bought by new people. That day she chose to ride Kangaroo, who sensed an opportunity to get even. Just as she reached the door, 'the girth slipped, flipping her under Kangaroo's side.'

Albert Hadley's taste was very different from Sister's. His summer house in Dark Harbor, a converted barn, was basically a white space into which he infused some subtle blues and browns.

He trotted off, depositing Sister in the village outside the shop, where, with as much dignity as could be mustered under such circumstances, she attempted to give a plausible explanation as to what had happened. She had actually broken her coccyx.[9]

Eventually Kangaroo was put out to grass and Sister, wisely deciding to go mechanical (machines don't bite or kick), bought a golf cart, which she would drive down the centre of the road as though it were a Sherman tank. She also kept a car on the island, which a young cousin who was designated chauffeur for a couple of years described as 'a horrible, junky little four-door Chevette hatchback'.[10] The 'small green clown car', as he characterized it, was in sharp contrast to the chauffeur-driven black Humber that was such a familiar sight around New York. In her later years in Maine she finally upgraded to an aubergine-coloured 1984 Cadillac Seville.

Sister also loved to swim in the freezing Maine waters, and to go boating. She owned a small blue speed boat which she would drive far too fast to some remote cove where an impromptu picnic would be held. Of course it is always a good idea to secure the mooring rope, but on one occasion she and Albert noticed the boat merrily drifting out to sea. Fortunately it was retrievable.

Snooping around other people's houses and swimming from other people's beaches passed the time, as did innumerable al fresco lunches, jolly cocktail parties, and convivial dinner parties. Sister was, of course, a mainstay of the Dark Harbor gossip mill, which was fairly laced with spite, malice and a small quantity of benevolence. To those who came to live on the island, usually as summer residents, she was generous with her invitations and her introductions. The highlight of the Dark Harbor 'season' was not some grand ball, but the annual dog show started by Sister's children, Apple and D.B., when Apple was ten years old. Sister's maid, Kusi, made the ribbons and Mr Haslum, the Marshall Fields' chauffeur (the Marshall Fields had a large house on the island), set out the ring. The first year the proceeds went to help repair the church gutters, while another year they helped to buy a font. The whole event gradually took on a life of its own.

The publication of the Summer House in 1967, and then again in 1971, caused quite a stir in decorating circles.

LEFT The annual dog show, the highlight of the Dark Harbor season. was held on the lawn of the Summer House.

RIGHT AND BELOW Sister loved driving around Dark Harbor with her grandchildren and her dogs, in the governess cart pulled by her cantankerous pony, Kangeroo.

BELOW LEFT TO RIGHT The Red House;
the Sister Parish Shop's handpainted
sign; planted baskets – always a
popular line.

The country look struck the right note and captured the public's imagination. In New York Sister always worked out of an office; unlike John Fowler in London, she never really had a shop. But Dark Harbor was different, and in the early 1970s Sister opened the Sister Parish Shop in the Red House. It was featured in *House & Garden* magazine in May 1973 – the photographs were taken the previous year – and in the article Sister explained that she had opened the shop to provide employment for her eight grandchildren. Her husband's explanation was rather different, and perhaps nearer the mark – his view was that she set up the shop 'because one day she had nothing to do for fifteen minutes'.[11] The enterprise involved her daughter Apple and granddaughter Susan and some local people who engaged in various crafts. They also sold things from considerably further afield, including fabrics from Tunis and Guatemala and rugs from Ireland. The rag rugs, made locally by Helen Gushie, were a particular favourite; these found their way even into the White House.

Sister's own particular craft was découpage. She loved to take old seed and farm catalogues, bird and flower books and anything else that came to hand, cut out whatever appealed. and glue the shapes on to card lampshades. Each cut-out, be it a bird or a butterfly or whatever, she would outline with pinpricks made using an old-fashioned ice pick. The effect when the lamps were lit was charming. She never worked out the design beforehand, merely used what she found and hoped for the best. If she wanted a glossy finish they would be given a coat of varnish.

She did from time to time use elements of country style in clients' houses, but usually only in light touches. Very few schemes where she did go the whole hog were photographed. There is, however, a record, in the shape of an article in *House & Garden* magazine, of one house in which Sister created some quite remarkable country style interiors. The clients were John Carter-Brown, who was, from 1969 until his retirement in 1992, Director of the National Gallery of Art in Washington, D.C., and his wife, Connie, a member of the Mellon family. They wanted a weekend retreat where the family could relax. An eighteenth-century farm cottage in the Pennsylvania countryside seemed the ideal place. The original house was tiny, so a new living room was added.

BELOW The interior of the Sister
Parish Shop. Sister made the
découpage lampshades herself.

BELOW Sister and her granddaughter Susan at work in the garden of the shop; and some of Sister's découpage lampshades.

RIGHT Sister painted the floor of the Summer House kitchen and filled the room with needlework pictures and brightly patterned rugs and cloths.

This room was an impressive 30 feet long. If the house had a theme it was 'early'; 'Everything [was] Early English, Early American, Early Indian – to keep in harmony with the house.'[12] Most of the objects were simple country pieces whose primary purpose was function rather than decorative beauty. It was probably the most 'rustic' decorative scheme Sister ever devised.

The oldest part of the house – what had been the original eighteenth-century sitting room and kitchen – became the day sitting room. Here there were Indian dhurries, lamps from the Far East, a wall hanging from Guatemala, allied with a quilted tablecloth and a knitted blanket from Maine. In the long living room, which served as the principal room, all was oak, whitewash and brick. Against this background Sister deployed an array of blues, pinks and mauves. The floor was strewn with kilims in bold geometric patterns, a theme picked up by the boldly patterned curtains with their simple pelmet, all of which were juxtaposed with a sofa and chair in a sophisticated chintz which had been hand-quilted in Kentucky. As one looks at the photographs today, nearly forty years later, what is immediately striking is the very formal arrangement of the room: it could almost be a Manhattan drawing room rather than a log cabin in the country – except that instead of Louis XV fauteuils Sister used simple Windsor and ladderback chairs, none of which seemed to match.

Downstairs was another sitting room, known as the den, and this was a favourite with Connie Carter-Brown. As she recalled, 'When I am in the house and guests arrive we always gravitate to this room,' with its welcoming apricot glow and its view to the Pennsylvania countryside. The room was another glorious mixture, from the Guatemalan lacquered coffee table to the English patterned carpet, the bold linen print curtains and the Indian baskets. 'By using artifacts and handcrafts,' as Sister remarked, 'we were able to keep the look of what it is – a country cabin.' The dining room was filled with good honest English oak. The lovely rush-seated ladderback chairs, each with a welcoming seat-pad, were actually a harlequin set. They were used with a simple round oak gate-leg table set upon a simple cotton dhurrie.

Only two of the bedrooms were photographed. The first was a guest room with English chintz curtains and tweed carpet. The twin beds had English black lacquer headboards which were decorated with country scenes, complemented by Early American bedspreads. In the master bedroom the bedspread, bed head and window curtains were crewelwork. The pinks and apricot colours were reflected in the dhurrie, and harmonized with the painted and lacquer furniture and an Early American corner cupboard. The old beams and rustic walls were on display – a deliberate ploy. 'We played it up wherever we could,' Sister remarked and as the *House & Garden* article concluded, 'This is the informal approach to living with the past – the distinguishing feature of this house.'[13]

These interiors were probably the only full-blown version of the American Country Style created by Sister, aside from her own homes, which were ever photographed and published. Looking at these interiors today, and those in her own homes, they are undeniably eccentric, yet they seem beautifully comfortable, and they have a quirky charm that remains enticing.

A PLACE
IN TOWN

The corridor at 39 East 79th Street. **PREVIOUS PAGES** Parish-Hadley 'Bolero' in beige.

A PLACE
IN TOWN

The first married home of Sister and Harry Parish was the house given to them as a dowry by Sister's parents, at 146 East End Avenue in the Yorkville area of New York, then a popular German-American district. These solid red brick town houses between East 86th and 87th Street, opposite Carl Schurz Park which fronts on to the East River, were built to designs by Lamb & Rich in 1899. Originally there were thirty-two houses in the development, but only twenty-four now remain. It was a decent-sized house with a drawing room and dining room and three bedrooms, plus accommodation for staff. It was decorated from top to bottom by Mrs Brown of McMillen's in the conventional taste of the period, and all Sister had to do was buy a chair (she got one from Macy's and was appalled that she had to pay $40 for it).[1]

During the Second World War Sister took an apartment at East 82nd Street, and after the war the Parishes lived in another apartment at 4 Sutton Place on the Lower East Side of New York. The apartment (it was probably a duplex) was never published in full, although a photograph of Harry's bedroom/library, here used as a dining room with a table set for a party of four, was illustrated in *Vogue* in March 1951. A large round book table became the dining table, while a French Louis XVI commode with its grey marble top served as a sideboard. This apartment consisted of just two bedrooms and a large drawing room, and after a few years they began looking for something larger.

They found a bigger apartment on the twelfth floor at 39 East 79th Street. Red brick with stone facings, the block was built in 1915 and became a very exclusive co-op building in 1925. Emily Post, author of *Etiquette: The Blue Book of Social Usage*, published in 1922, lived in the building from 1928 until her death in 1960.[2] The Parishes' apartment was essentially four rooms – two bedrooms, a dining room and drawing room. The end wall of the tiny square vestibule was covered in an antique mirror, which made the gallery that opened off it appear longer than it actually was. Painted bamboo fretwork decorated the walls and ceiling, and an iron version of a bamboo lantern carried on the chinoiserie theme. The gallery, which led past the bedrooms to the drawing room at the far end, was adorned by panels of Japanese wallpaper with a tea-coloured background. Along its length stood a group of Louis XVI chairs that

BELOW LEFT Harry's bedroom at the Sutton Place apartment, arranged as a dining room.

BOTTOM LEFT AND RIGHT The drawing room at 39 East 79th Street after its 1968 makeover. Glazed chocolate-brown walls, chalk-white silk damask, cream satin and an old French chintz *à la chinoise* combined with a red lacquer coffee table.

retained their original needlework coverings, and by the drawing room door stood a Boulle cabinet that acted as the drinks cabinet.

The drawing room was a large, glamorous room some 27 × 19 feet with a range of windows facing due south and further single windows flanking the fireplace facing east. The room's decoration revolved around a large Aubusson rug and simple silk curtains. The sofas and chairs were covered in a variety of fabrics, but in the summer, when the Aubusson left for its annual clean and repair, they were all 'slip covered in a cotton material printed in sepia and off-white vermicelli pattern'.[3] A few photographs of the apartment appeared over the years, and the apartment as a whole featured in an article with the title 'The Taste for the Cherishable', which appeared in *House Beautiful* in October 1968. Sister had recently given the drawing room a makeover that included chocolate-brown walls, which had been glazed so they had a 'wet-gleaming look'. She contrasted this with sofas in chalk-white silk damask, chairs in cream satin, and a French chintz *à la chinoise* used on yet another sofa.[4]

The dining room opened off the drawing room and, although at 15 × 14 feet it was not a large room, it was resplendent, with Italian painted wall panels in shades of soft green and cream. Around the small mahogany table was a set of Louis XVI painted chairs that had belonged to Sister's parents (it came from the apartment they kept in Paris in the 1920s), while above hung a pretty eighteenth-century 'crystal confection' from Italy. Mark Hampton remembered lunching there with one of Sister's friends. He had come to New York to buy an engagement ring. Sister and her friend thought that a very amusing thing to do. 'What a stupid idea,' Sister told him, 'I sold mine to buy a horse.' Her friend confided, 'My husband pawned mine to pay a gambling debt' – whose debt she did not reveal, and no one was indelicate enough to ask.[5]

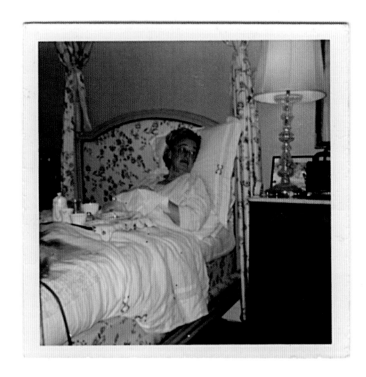

In Sister's own bedroom, the walls were painted a soft apricot and the *polonaise* bed was dressed with 'a print of her own design' (possibly done with Albert Hadley). An antique quilt served as a bedspread. Harry's bedroom does not seem to have been photographed, but when they moved its decoration was copied exactly in the new apartment.

In the early 1970s Harry's doctor advised that he should spend as much time as possible in Maine, where the air was far clearer than in heavily polluted New York. He suffered from long-standing chest problems. In the light of this it seemed sensible that they should give up the large East 79th Street apartment. Sister started to look for a new apartment, and was rather depressed by what was on offer. And then Providence took a hand. One day she was walking home on Fifth Avenue when she spotted, quite by chance, a door ajar on the corner of 77th Street. Being naturally nosy, she had a peek and discovered that the apartment had high ceilings, 'the entrance hall was marble, the cornice was of great quality, and . . . the living room was square – my favourite shape for a room.'[6] Never a woman to hang around, Sister determined then and there that she wanted the apartment, 'even if I had to murder the tenant' to get her hands on it. The doorman was the soul of discretion and would not reveal to whom the apartment belonged. Undeterred, Sister staked out

the place every afternoon until 'I caught the owner, a lovely lady, walking in the front door.' Sister accosted her – 'she looked at me as if I were demented' – but she allowed her to see the whole apartment. It was very small by comparison with 79th Street and they would definitely need one more room, but Sister worked out that if she blocked up the door to the street she could create a tiny bedroom some 5 feet wide by 9 feet long where the entrance lobby had been. The 'lovely lady' was prepared to sell, and Sister bought it. She was thrilled with her new apartment.

There was a tiny entrance vestibule from the apartment block corridor. This opened into what had been the hall, a good almost square space but with no windows. Sister turned it into a dining room, covering the walls with a white sisal square-patterned vinyl. The floor was black and white tile, laid on the diamond, but the ceiling was done in a deep reddish orange. A Japanese lantern became the chandelier, and a tall wooden sculpture of a duck sat on the table beneath. Above a small painted console table was a modern painting, while pine corner cabinets stood guard on either side. This led, via an arched opening, into the living room. Doors on the immediate right led to Harry's bedroom – which had been copied exactly from his bedroom in the 79th Street apartment – and to the house bathroom.

FAR LEFT In the dining room *trompe l'oeil* panelling from a villa in the Veneto was combined with eighteenth-century French furniture, some of which had been in her parents' Paris apartment.

LEFT AND BELOW Sister's bedroom at East 79th Street. The bed is hung with a print of her own design, which sets the colour theme for the room.

Another door on the extreme left opened into Sister's broom closet bedroom, into which she somehow managed to cram, as well as her bed, masses of tiny pictures, a screen, a chandelier, a mirror, a chair and a closet created where a radiator had once stood.

In the living room, which was some 18 × 21 feet, she lifted the height of the door to 9 feet, to give the room more grandeur. And it was here she had her modernist moment: a sort of later-life teenage rebellion. Partly in an effort to be modern, and partly to make the apartment easy to run, she covered the living room walls with plum-coloured vinyl. The aubergine colour made the room appear larger than it actually was, and the unusual finish meant it could be easily washed down. Today it sounds perfectly ghastly, but in the early 1970s such finishes were all the rage. (Fortunately the rage didn't last long.) The floor was good herringbone parquet, so this was bleached and polished and then strewn with rugs, notably a large pale patterned linen rug from a nineteenth-century Indian summer palace. Its pattern of birds, flowers and horses – some with riders and some not – brought an echo of country style into the centre of Manhattan. For curtains Sister used a heavy cotton basket-weave pattern in mauve and white that was edged with orange. This colour combination seems to have been inspired by a shell picked up on the beach in Dark Harbor.

Sister brought the furniture from her old drawing room, but she filled the room with ornaments, had lamps of white plaster, and echoed the modern theme in the fabrics she chose. On a French fauteuil, which she painted white, she used an abstract pattern designed by Alan Campbell, and she used another Campbell fabric for cushions on a sofa. The white cotton chaise longue in the far corner of the room was piled with zigzag-patterned cushions and a six-colour Indian throw, all of which lived happily with the Campbell prints. In her view, 'There were no ornaments except the essentials. It really was an almost empty, very pure room.' Only, of course, it wasn't: Sister might have kept a lot of her ornaments packed away in boxes, but it still seemed that every surface was covered by bibelots. It was almost a contradiction in terms: a modernist room full of pattern and texture. Sister was forced to concede, 'It wasn't me. I felt out of place in it and never truly comfortable. I kept sneaking back into Harry's room, with its old blue-and-white chintz where I'd curl up on his sofa under his wonderful tattered old quilt. This was my idea of home.'[7]

But she wasn't yet prepared to give up on being 'modern'. She sought Albert's advice and he suggested she needed to be a bit more 'racy' and 'jazzy'. He advised her to buy some modern art, to partly mirror one wall using mirror tiles, and to cover the ceiling with silver-leaf Chinese

tea paper, a trick he had learnt from A. Herbert Rodgers. The changes were implemented, and new curtains made in a shocking shade of magenta, while she was away on a job: 'When I came back, I walked into the room and nearly fainted dead away. The curtains were flaming magenta! I felt Albert had made me into Mae West – on my stage. "Take those hideous things down at once!" I said "By morning."'[8]

Dawn did not come for well over a year. Secretly she got a lot of pleasure from the shock the contrast gave, and she felt some of her friends were embarrassed by the juxtaposition. But when the novelty value had dissipated, Sister redecorated the room in a more traditional manner. Out went the aubergine-coloured vinyl and in came a French moiré wallpaper with blue and white stripes separated by a thin gold line. In came a fine English Axminster rug and favourite old chintzes once more covered the furniture. The flaming magenta gave way to pale blue silk curtains and finally all the boxes of ornaments were unpacked. The rebellion was over. There was one last change. The silver tea

paper on the ceiling inexplicably turned a pale gold colour, which seemed to fit the new decorative scheme perfectly.

Sister moved one last time, to a slightly larger apartment at 920 Fifth Avenue which had once been actress Gloria Swanson's New York home. This had the huge advantage of a tiny garden. In her new drawing room she papered the walls in a wide stripe-on-stripe design, and covered the sofas in white damask. The blue silk curtains came with her from 960 Fifth Avenue to be remade and reused. A large oval English Axminster carpet (some 17 × 13 feet) in a neoclassical pattern helped consolidate the rather pale scheme. A pair of bergère chairs were covered in her favourite chintz, 'Floral Bouquet' by Lee Jofa, as were another two painted bergères and various *fauteuils en cabriolet*. Many of the objects she used are familiar from her other apartments, while some, such as the Queen Anne mirror and the pair of George III gilt three-light girandoles, she had inherited from her parents. All was gilt, painted or lacquer, with scarcely a piece of brown furniture to be seen.

LEFT In the living room of 960 Fifth Avenue, Sister in modern mode. On the aubergine-coloured vinyl, a striking modern painting is juxtaposed with a pair of English girandoles that reflect the curtains. On the floor is a patterned linen rug from an Indian summer palace.

RIGHT Sister's last drawing room, at 920 Fifth Avenue, where she returned to a traditional style.

145

Opening from the drawing room was the smaller sitting room, with walls the colour of lobster bisque. The room was dominated by the pair of painted wooden valances, their shape formed by two ogee arches, edged by a fringe and terminated by a large wooden tassel. The pale olive green background contrasted with the walls and was picked up by a nineteenth-century painted writing table and by the chinoiserie-decorated painted panels which she used as large pictures. Here painted and lacquer furniture was freely mixed with brown furniture, including a beautiful Queen Anne walnut bureau bookcase that had once been in her father's collection.

Opening off the small entrance hall, which Sister got the painter to do with hand-painted stripes of blue on a creamy background and topped by a swagged paper border, was the dining room. She covered the walls with 'Urn and Bouquet' chintz wallpaper from Rose Cumming and used the same chintz to upholster the ebonized dining chairs, filling the room with pattern and making it appear larger than it actually was. Her bedroom, with its over-scaled four-poster dressed in chintz and linen, as David Kleinberg pointed out, 'exemplifies the Parish style'.[9] Pretty pieces of painted furniture filled the room, while her bathroom, the walls papered in a small-flowered chintz, was more like a cosy sitting room.

ABOVE Sister and Bunny Williams, in fancy dress at one of Sister's parties.

LEFT The entrance hall of Sister's last apartment. The blue stripes were hand-painted on the wall.

BELOW The dining room walls were papered in 'Urn and Bouquet' and the same pattern and the same pattern was used for the chair covers.

BELOW RIGHT Sister's bedroom, filled with pretty painted furniture, was light and charming. The bedspread was made from a chintz by Cowtan & Tout, while the curtains, the bed hangings and some of the upholstery were in a Sanderson fabric.

The Summer House in Maine, the house that exemplified American Country Style, was Sister's home. The New York apartments were more transitory, owned for no more than ten years before she moved on, no doubt playing the real estate market and selling for a substantial profit. These too reflected a very distinctive style. This was a look clearly inspired by the English Country House Style developed by her friend Nancy Lancaster and John Fowler, but there were marked differences. In particular, this American version of Country House Style included far more references to France than one would find in England: this was perhaps natural considering American history, with its rejection of all things British following the revolution of 1776. Sister's colours were far brighter and crisper than those used in the English Country House Style; this reflected the different quality of the light. The cashmere throws so often found on sofas – not something that would have appeared in a London drawing decorated by John Fowler – were a sensible response to the cold New York winter evenings. Sister was an incessant entertainer and she usually entertained at home, so many had the opportunity, while drinking her bourbon and eating her canapés, to admire her rooms. Spreading further, almost all these apartments were published, and on several occasions, so they were seen and had a huge influence on other decorators and the public at large. Indeed, Mario Buatta use to ring Sister up and ask 'What have you done recently that I can copy?' This was only half meant in jest. It was a look, a style and a level of luxury the East Coast rich admired and aspired to for themselves. In her work Sister gave them a version of the look, often euphemistically called the 'undecorated look'. In reality it was anything but.

Sister Parish's Bedroom

DESIGNS FOR LIVING

The famous red lacquer library in Brooke Astor's apartment at 778 Park Avenue. This was perhaps the most famous room created by Parish-Hadley.

PREVIOUS PAGES Parish-Hadley 'Parish Stripe'.

DESIGNS FOR LIVING

P arish-Hadley Inc. developed into quite a large firm. Sister always thought she was on the edge of ruin: as one of her friends commented, 'The trouble with Sister is her clients are all so rich that she thinks automatically of herself as poor.' By comparison with some of her clients she was as poor as the proverbial church mouse. But her business grossed several million dollars a year, though there was 'a staff of twenty-four to support', and, of course, 'Uncle Sam swallows our profits.' Sister loved to plead poverty, near destitution, one step from the workhouse, as she elegantly stepped into her chauffeur-driven puce Buick, the successor to the old Humbers she used to be driven around in.[1]

Though Sister was often described as creating the 'undecorated' look, to characterize her and her work thus was quite misleading. As she remarked 'If there is a theme to my work, it is the theme of my life – continuity.' This idea of continuity, of a link to the past, was the basis of everything Sister did and it is why her partnership with Albert Hadley was so successful. Albert Hadley was, basically, 'a modernist mugged by nostalgia'. He and Sister in effect faced in opposite directions: he forward to the bright new world, and she back to the rich glow of the past. Like Nancy Lancaster and John Fowler in England, Sister never followed trends or fashions for she, like they, 'believed as I do now, that rooms should be timeless and very personal. I don't set out to achieve a particular style. And I certainly don't have a "look" – just a mishmash of everything that somehow, by instinct, usually turns out to be warm, imaginative, "living" room.'[2] Houses live and breathe and also reflect. They should be in accord with the personality of the owner and also with their own architecture, style and period. Sister believed it was 'bad manners for a room to look pretentious', as Mark Hampton remarked.

For all Sister's fame as a decorator, like Nancy Lancaster she wasn't really interested in decorating. She actually took a rather dim view of the decorating world in general, and many decorators in particular. She was appalled at the chatter of the 'young people' she would overhear in the Decorators' Building in New York (usually in the elevator). She would listen to them waffling away about styles and trends, knowing all the time that 'they'll never do anything the least bit

attractive', and that they were the reason 'there have to be so many hideous things on sale in the building'. She was, quite rightly, 'appalled at what American taste really is today. Alas, the very worst is often the most expensive.'

Sister continued to choose her clients with care. And she was wise to do so. If there is no sympathy between decorator and client this tension is usually revealed in the work, which is never satisfactory. On the other hand, if there is a rapport and an understanding this, too, is usually evident in the end result. A work created with feeling, harmony and (dare one say) love is always far superior to one created with rancour, mistrust and mutual loathing. Once accepted, clients would find themselves subjected to the indignity of the 'tea trolley' – Sister would push a tea trolley around their room, consigning everything deemed unsuitable to its ample shelves. She could usually fill it quite easily.

Of course, sometimes a small detail can reveal a hidden desire and produce an empathy. Summoned to look at a house near Boston on her way up to Maine, Sister was searching for something pleasant to say, and busily composing a nice letter of rejection in her mind. Everything was hideous, and the house quite ugly. However, in a bathroom she spotted a small multicoloured bathmat and remarked what a pretty mat it was. 'Well,' said the owner, 'that's the look I really would like to have.' She hadn't been able to explain, but what she really wanted was an American Country Style house. She and her husband became one of Sister's most appreciative clients. As Sister remarked, their tastes developed and matured to the point where they 'probably know more than I do about crafts'.[3]

In the late 1960s Sister was asked to work on an apartment in Boston for the Rabb family, who owned the grocery store chain 'Stop and Shop' (known locally as the 'Stop and Pee'). The apartment was just a shell when the Rabbs acquired it. Albert created the spaces. Perhaps the most dramatic is the drawing room. Opening off the hall, this room is an essay in pared-down classicism. There are large windows looking out to the river and to the common, which makes the room very light. What comes as a surprise today is that the walls are a deep chocolate brown, with a frieze of triglyphs (a Doric moulding) picked out in mushroom and white. But chocolate brown was a very popular colour in the late 1960s. Billy Baldwin used it often.

Sister used a central circular table to divide the room in two. The fireplace was at one end, while opposite was the largest window overlooking the river. Here she placed a large low sofa, flanked by French chairs with a low coffee table between. The other two windows, dressed with simple curtains in a beige and white abstract design, were separated by a large lacquered cabinet. Opposite this, against the chocolate-brown walls Sister placed a large sofa upholstered in chocolate-brown silk. Again there were more chairs, this time in a yellow stripe fabric, all set on a striped parquet floor similar to that in the hall. It was, in essence, a chocolate drawing room. Opening off was the smaller dining room, but here the walls were dragged yellow and orange. Yellow was used again for the small library also looking out across the river. When the Rabbs moved out the apartment was bought by Sister's niece, who also bought some of the furnishings and added to them what she already had, also created by Sister. So what we see today is a kind of hybrid: decorated for one client and furnished for another.

One of Sister's most faithful clients was her old friend Brooke Astor. These houses form an interesting collection of interiors all decorated around one person. They also reflect a way of life that has now all but ceased to exist.

Sister and Brooke Astor first worked together at Astor Courts, Ferncliff, in the 1950s (see pages 34–5). Brooke continued to live at Ferncliff until 1965. In the early 1960s, however, she moved her New York home from 120 East End Avenue (at 85th Street) to 778 Park Avenue. This apartment became one of Parish-Hadley's most famous projects.

Designed by Rosario Candela, 778 Park Avenue was constructed in 1931. Brooke Astor's apartment was on the sixteenth and fifteenth floors, with most of the principal rooms facing south-east. The elevators opened into a small private hall and then into the gallery, a long, low corridor with a barrel-vaulted ceiling. Sister treated this as an architectural space, painting it a rich cream and being careful not to over-furnish it.

A pair of lacquered doors (two panels from a Chinese screen) opened into the dining room, which was a fairly substantial room some 26 × 20 feet. Above the Louis XV fireplace hung a fine Chippendale chinoiserie mirror, and this set the theme for the room. The skirting and dado panels were marbled in greys, picking up the colour of the marble fireplace, but the walls above were a deep green, broken by large eighteenth-century murals by Jean Pillement in pink on an off-white ground. The furniture was mostly French, and included a set of Louis XV chairs and a simple mahogany extending table. The two windows overlooking Park Avenue were elaborately dressed. There were simple white voile inner curtains to diffuse the light but the main curtains were in pink taffeta, picking up the colour of the murals, with swag draperies trimmed by a pleated edge. The over-draperies were of deep green silk, tied by large bows as the silk cascaded to the floor. There was no chandelier, and usually the dining room was lit by candlelight, but the ceiling had the addition of a discreet boxing which contained tiny lights that were trained on the murals. At the time this was considered a very modern idea.

ABOVE The gallery at 778 Park Avenue, looking through into the dining room.

RIGHT The dining room. The eighteenth-century pink and white murals were bought in France.

The drawing room next door was of comparable size but far lighter than the dining room, for there were four large windows facing on to Park Avenue. Done in a pale cream – a sort of buttermilk colour – the room was planned around the early nineteenth-century English Axminster carpet. Its colours were reflected in the chintz (Cowtan and Tout's 'Bouquet Anglaise') used for the curtains and to upholster some of the chairs, plus cushions on the three sofas arranged around the room. The curtain draperies were quite elaborate – swags with tails and bells, with frilled edging in pink silk which also ran down the leading edge of the curtains: a decidedly John Fowler touch. The

sofas were covered in Quadrille's 'Shalimar', in tones of beige so they did not force themselves upon the eye. The pictures were mostly old master drawings. Pieces of lacquer furniture, lamps and the garniture on the mantelpiece picked up the chinoiserie theme.

Lacquer was the dominant feature in the library, which opened off the drawing room and gallery to the south. The original library had French panelling, as was the fashion at the time it was built. When Brooke Astor tired of this and wanted something different, Albert Hadley conceived the idea of a red lacquer library. Three walls were given over to a range of floor to ceiling shelves, edged by a brass trim

LEFT Panels from a Chinese lacquer screen were used as doors opening from the gallery into the dining room.

BELOW The pale drawing room. The looking glass came from the library at Astor Courts.

that defined the composition. The small French fireplace (probably originally meant for a bedroom) was flanked by two pairs of mirrored doors leading into the drawing room and the gallery respectively. The sofa and chairs from the old library, covered in a Brunschwig fabric, 'La Portugaise', and the old Bessarabian rug were returned so there was both innovation and continuity; the familiar juxtaposed with the new. It was a huge success, and it became the most photographed room in New York.

Opening off the gallery was a short corridor that ran at the back of the library and led to Brooke's writing room. Painted in soft apricot, the walls of this room were hung with numerous glass pictures of Chinese scenes. The corridor turned west past what had once been a bedroom, but was now the blue sitting room, its walls hung with blue moiré (Brunschwig's 'Ravel'). A pretty English Adam mirror hung above a sofa, surrounded by a small collection of watercolours of oriental scenes – continuing the chinoiserie theme. The corridor continued to Brooke's bedroom on the building's west corner. Here the *lit à la polonaise* she had brought from Ferncliff was redressed in a light flowery print in pinks and greens set on a cream ground. The print was used everywhere – for the bed, for the window curtains, on a chaise and a chair, and also as the wallpaper. The floor was painted with a design of diamonds, but much of it was covered by a plain neutral rug. It was a light, pretty and very feminine room.

In the mid-1960s (probably 1965) Brooke Astor gave the Rhinebech estate to the Roman Catholic Church, and at the suggestion of Nelson Rockefeller she bought Holly Hill, at Briarcliff Manor. The house was in Pocantico Hills, thirty miles from New York. It became Brooke Astor's favourite home, and it was here that she died in August 2007 aged 105. The house had been designed by Billy Delano of the New York architects Delano & Aldrich. It was airy and light, but also full of American comfort.

ABOVE Brooke's writing room. Glass
pictures hang on the apricot walls.

OPPOSITE ABOVE The blue sitting room.

OPPOSITE BELOW Brooke's
bedroom, with the *lit à la polonaise*
she brought from Ferncliff.

At Holly Hill the drawing room, some 42 feet long with a wide bay window, gave wonderful views to the terrace gardens and rolling hills in the distance. Delano's panelling, which was loosely based on eighteenth-century French *boiseries*, was painted a good solid cream, with a paler shade used for the cornice and slightly paler again for the ceiling. A yellow silk taffeta was chosen for the curtains, and the colour was also used on some of the French chairs and as cushions on the four sofas. Two of the sofas were in ivory damask and two in a chintz that was also used for some of the other French chairs and again as cushions. With four sofas and no less than ten chairs the room should have seemed cluttered but, on the contrary, it worked beautifully.

The dining room beyond was again decorated in the French taste. The walls were papered with wallpaper in alternating flat and lustrous stripes in two different shades of grey. The ceiling was a very soft grey, a colour that had been devised by Nancy Lancaster for the dining room at

Ditchley before the war and that she christened 'elephant's breath'. There was a panelled library and what had been the old morning room became the 'memory room', lined with photographs of Brooke Astor and her late husband and numerous trinkets of sentimental value. The bottle-green walls made the perfect background for the accumulations of a life, and the bold, bright sofa fabric brought vitality to the room.

In the summer Brooke would go to Cove End, her house in Northeast Harbor on Mount Desert Island in Maine. By Maine summer cottage standards Cove End, which was built for Barton Eddison by Roger Griswold and Millard Gulick of the architects Little & Russell, is a modest house.[4] Vincent Astor bought it in 1953, the year he and Brooke were married. As she recalled, the first summer after their marriage 'was spent in Europe, motoring and yachting. We both hated it, and it was a glorious moment when we decided that we both loved Maine.'[5]

ABOVE The sun room, overlooking part of the garden.

RIGHT The sweeping staircase lined by Brooke's collection of dog paintings.

In 1963 Brooke asked Sister to redecorate Cove End, which she did, working around the fine collection of New England country furniture which the Astors had bought with the house. This was among the first jobs Albert Hadley did with Sister. He drew meticulous floor plans, just as he had been trained to do, and everything had a precise location decided well in advance in the office. Installation day dawned and, as he recalled, 'We were both in Maine when the delivery truck finally arrived with all the furniture. With her propelling them, tables and chairs scooted across the floor in an entirely different configuration from my plans. This was the first time I had actually witnessed Sis's baroque, freewheeling style of working. I was completely entranced.'[6]

The large living room was painted in a cheery yellow, with curtains of blue linen that had a wide braid along the leading edge. The blue was picked up by a bold blue and green chintz used on a number of chairs, while the sofas were in a deep cream with a large mauve diamond pattern. These large, comfortable sofas had been designed by Stanford White for the sports complex at Ferncliff, where they stood around the swimming pool.

In all these houses and apartments Sister created a setting for Brooke Astor's life. As Sister's granddaughter recalled, 'Briarcliff, New York, stands out as the scene of colourful verbal skirmishes between Mrs Astor and Sister, both very competitive women. It was also the most representative of a way of life we don't see anymore.' Going to lunch was a treat. The door 'would be opened by the familiar major domo of the house, whom my grandmother knew well as she visited often.'[7] The familiar cry of 'hoo hoo' received the also familiar echo of 'we are in here', meaning the large drawing room or the smaller library. To a young person the whole scene seemed like a world frozen in time.

For all her wealth, however, Brooke Astor was not really an extravagant woman and many of Sister's clients lived in a far grander manner than she did. The Whitneys were an example. 'Jock' Whitney and his second wife, Betsey, had seven houses, and they filled them all with wonderful paintings. They had a large town house in New York at East 63rd Street (but latterly they lived in a duplex on Beekman Place); Greentree, a large country house at Manhasset on Long Island set in over 500 acres; a smaller

house at Saratoga Springs, New York State; a summer house on Fishers' Island; a golf cottage in Augusta; Greenwood, a famous old plantation house in southern Georgia set in 19,000 acres; plus a flat in Grosvenor Square in London, across the road from the American Embassy.

Although Sister knew the Whitneys socially, she did not work for them until the mid-1960s. The town house at 63rd Street was built after the Second World War and up on the roof the Whitneys decided to create a modern room which was intended as a sort of private domain. To the south were sliding glass doors facing the street, while to the north lay the garden (conveniently, Jock Whitney owned the houses opposite, so could do what he liked). When Sister went to look at the space the room was bare, with white walls, a Moroccan rug and Barcelona chairs. It just wasn't the Whitneys' style. They hated it. One idea had been to do a trellis room, but perhaps that was a bit of a cliché. Walking round the block Sister saw a van unloading some old shutters, which had once been painted but the paint had flaked off, leaving that look old worn pine manages to achieve and is impossible to fake. She bought half of them there and then. When she took one of these old pine shutters with its peeling paint back to show the Whitneys, Betsey

immediately grasped the point. By some miracle the shutters fitted perfectly. The room now had a theme. Sister had the walls painted white, then covered in heavy linen canvas which was painted a crusty white. Bookshelves flanking the beige and white Italian chimneypiece were painted mustard yellow. Betsy and Sister retained a large blue and white dhurrie in a geometric pattern for the floor and covered two large sofas and numerous chairs in blue and white patterned linen, and others in plain linen. Finally at one end of the room, Sister placed a narrow gothic bookcase to balance a large Rousseau landscape on the opposite wall. Betsey Whitney had her special room.

From then on the Whitneys frequently used the services of Parish-Hadley. They worked at Greentree, the Whitney estate at Manhasset, Long Island, when the guest wing – which hadn't been used for years – had to be spruced up for a visit from Princess Margaret and Lord Snowdon. They were to spend four days there in September, and it was already May. The guest wing opened off a corridor or gallery that was maybe 100 feet long and 10 feet wide and full of all those bits and pieces of family memorabilia which never really find a home anywhere else in a house. The guest rooms themselves, which were seldom used, were

LEFT The Whitneys' 'modern room' at their New York town house. Sister found the shutters being unloaded from a truck round the corner and bought half the load on the spot.

RIGHT ABOVE The living room at Saratoga Springs, decorated around a rose-coloured chintz from Baily & Griffin.

RIGHT BELOW A guest bedroom at Saratoga Springs, an easy mix of chintz and needlework. The wallpaper was from Rose Cumming.

ABOVE Princess Margaret's bedroom at Greentree, the Whitney mansion at Manhasset, Long Island.

RIGHT Greenwood, the Whitneys' plantation house in southern Georgia, was entirely redecorated by Parish-Hadley. Sadly, the work had hardly been completed when the house was gutted by fire.

large and had good-sized windows looking over the garden towards the park beyond. The bathrooms had wonderful old-fashioned fittings – all white tiles, enormous bath tubs and chunky chrome. The job came together more quickly than at first seemed possible. The first room was decorated for Lord Snowdon. They used an old four-poster bed, which had been Jock Whitney's when he was a child, retaining the existing red damask hangings. The walls were covered in burlap painted off-white – sort of the colour of putty. Next they created a sitting room. It was painted a strong yellow and filled with black lacquer and papier mâché, together with a few more fancy pieces and an Empire sofa upholstered in striped chintz with flowers. The curtains were in pink and white striped silk taffeta, apparently hung from Victorian valances festooned with flowers – the valances were actually made from pressed tin.

The room where Princess Margaret was to sleep was next to the sitting room and by breaking through a closet they linked the two rooms to make a suite. The Princess's room was chosen for her because it was papered in a lovely nineteenth-century French wallpaper of a Boston scene by Zuber. It seemed appropriate to decorate the room following a Regency theme, and hunting around the house they found a lovely old Regency dressing table and some white and gold American Regency chairs. The curtains were made from the thinnest embroidered mull and were held back by Regency brass tie-backs. Albert found the Empire valance, and the curtains were 'caught up again with big brass buttons that went into the wall and then draped from there'.[8]

The Whitneys lived in some style. One Parish-Hadley decorator recalled going with Sister to lunch to be served 'lobster as our first course, tongue as our second course, and some amazing pastry. And there were footmen – could there have been three footmen ?'[9]

Eventually Parish-Hadley decorated the whole of the Greentree house. They also did the small house at Saratoga Springs, which the Whitneys kept just for the racing in August. This was done in more of a country style, as befitted

T—17 GREENWOOD PLANTATION, THOMASVILLE, GA.

E-6025

its more modest nature. The big blue front door opened into a spacious entrance hall with a black and white tile floor dominated by a large hexagonal table with a quilted cloth covered in bronzes. Sister used simple creamy white walls to which she added a scalloped paper border as a cornice. She continued the border into the sitting room beyond, again in a creamy white, but bedecked with a lovely chintz used as curtains and for some of the upholstery. Much of the furniture wasn't at all grand, but simple country pieces that seemed to live harmoniously with one another and the occasional grand piece of art. Betsey Whitney's bedroom carried on this simple theme with coordinated wallpaper and curtains, but the star of the room was the metal lacquer *polonaise* bed. Save for a poplin back curtain tied with bows, the bed was left 'undressed'.

Like so many plantations in the south, Greenwood, the family's house in southern Georgia, could be described as like something out of *Gone with the Wind*. This was especially appropriate, as Jock Whitney had put up half the money to buy the film rights of *Gone with the Wind* and he eventually owned the rights outright. Greenwood, with its huge Doric portico, was described by Stanford White as the finest example of a Greek Revival house in America. The house was set among magnolias, and the magnolia flower was the house emblem. Sister and Albert began (in the 1960s) by rearranging the house, which was a little threadbare and down at heel. They moved furniture around, doing most of the humping about themselves. Everything needed to be reupholstered, which they gradually did, and with the exception of a 'character chair' for the sitting room they bought no new furniture.

Parish-Hadley entirely redid the house in the 1980s. One of the decorators recalled going down with Sister, who was then quite elderly. In the early evening the staff came

LEFT The hall of the Paleys' Fifth Avenue apartment.

RIGHT The drawing room of the apartment was painted taxicab yellow.

and closed all the curtains. Dinner was served in the large dining room, with its huge Italian chandelier made from iron flowers, the candles flickering against the tangerine-coloured walls. Betsey Whitney, glittering in diamonds and emeralds, was almost more splendid than the room. After dinner the decorator retired to the guest lodge, to be woken some hours later by the fire alarm. Rushing around to the front of the house, he found Betsey Whitney and Sister in their nightdresses being helped down the front steps. They were fortunate: had they stayed in the house only a few more minutes both would have died of smoke inhalation. Henryk de Kwiatkowski, the aviation billionaire, sent a plane down to whisk these two elderly ladies to Long Island so neither would see the devastation the next morning. Sister was already frail, as was Betsey Whitney, and neither of them lived to see Greenwood restored to its former glory.

Given Sister's connections, it is hardly surprising that she also worked for Bill and Barbara (Babe) Paley. Babe Paley was the youngest of the three Cushing sisters. Her eldest sister was Betsey Whitney, while the second sister was Minnie, who had been married to Vincent Astor before he married Brooke. Bill's first wife had been Dorothy Hearst, whom he married in 1932 (they divorced in 1947), and they had been frequent guests at Ditchley Park in England. Indeed Bill was Michael Tree's oldest friend.

The Paleys had a superb art collection, as well as furniture of the highest quality. Bunny Williams recalled being sent around to the Fifth Avenue apartment with some samples. She rang the bell, which was answered by the butler; behind him was hanging a Picasso painting of a boy with a pony. The butler, seeing her interest, invited her in to look at the pictures. A large entrance hall opened into the drawing room, which Sister had painted in 'taxicab yellow'.

The room was panelled in antique *boiseries* based on those at the Hôtel Carnavalet in Paris: 'six different shades were needed as a base – plus glazing.' The painter was camped out there for five months.[10] By placing a Boulle table at right angles between the windows, Sister broke up the room so she could create three seating groups, each of which included a sofa covered in a dull satin with a variety of chairs in a mixture of other fabrics. The floor was strewn with brown dyed goat skin, cut into 2-foot-square pieces which were then sewn together. To tie the whole thing together Sister used tall Chinese red lacquer screens in two corners, reflected in the eighteenth-century English pier glass over the chimneypiece.

The Paleys had numerous other homes. Parish-Hadley worked at Kiluna Farm on Long Island, and also at what had been Eleanor Brown's (of McMillen's) old home at Southampton on Long Island. A room that been designed by Archibald Brown as a private theatre was converted in 1942 into a grand living room. Some 40 feet square and with a 22-foot ceiling, the room was of majestic proportions. The Paleys turned it into a grand reception room which Parish-Hadley decorated in a soft apricot. Sister, famed for her skill at arranging furniture, was able to assemble no less than seven separate groups.

One magazine editor described the apartment Sister decorated for Enid Haupt as the finest in New York. Mrs Haupt and her brother, Walter Annenberg, both had wonderful collections of Impressionist and Post-Impressionist paintings, which eventually they united (the Haupt and the Annenberg collections are now in the Metropolitan Museum in New York). Packed off to the care of her brother, Mrs Haupt's Impressionists were replaced by eighteenth-century frescoes brought from a Venetian palace. So a totally new look was required.

The large living room of the Paleys' house at Southampton, Long Island.

In the same room, a charming dining area looking out over a rill in the garden.

LEFT The library of Enid
Haupt's New York apartment,
decorated to convey what
Mrs Haupt called 'a *café au
lait* feeling'.

ABOVE RIGHT A corner of the
sitting/dining room, with Italian
drawings on the walls.

BELOW RIGHT The entrance
hall, with sweeping staircase,
marbled walls and unlined silk
taffeta curtains.

As Mrs Haupt explained, 'I'd never used a decorator before. . . . I'd never even had curtains. I just had plants, plants, plants – and the paintings. But I'd always said to Sister socially, "If I ever do a new scene, will you help me?"'[11] In the drawing room the once white walls became a sort of buttermilk colour, a perfect foil for the frescoes and the eighteenth-century furniture. Sister covered the French sofa and many of the chairs in her favourite chintz from Lee Jofa. In the centre was the 'roundabout' (an upholstered Victorian ottoman) inspired by the one in Nancy Lancaster's saloon at Haseley Court (although Sister would vehemently deny that she'd copied the idea from Haseley). In the library beyond, Enid Haupt wanted a '*café au lait*' feeling, so Parish-Hadley used pale walnut furniture and a Bessarabian rug. One visiting executive from the Metropolitan was moved to confess, 'People would be shocked to hear this but I like it better without the modern paintings,' to which Mrs Haupt replied 'But so do I.'[12]

Although the primary focus of Parish-Hadley was on domestic work, there were occasional forays into the commercial world. In the early 1970s they decorated the directors' suite for the Bank of New York.[13] The project was really under Albert's control and Sister had little input: photographs show the rooms to be in a modern idiom. They were also responsible for decorating the Ritz-Carlton Hotel in New York and in Boston. Sister undertook this work with Harold Simmons as her assistant. Sister was in Maine when John Bennett Coleman telephoned her and asked her to decorate the New York Ritz-Carlton. Hotels were not really her thing, so she hesitated but agreed to meet Coleman on her return to New York. Playing his hand with skill, Coleman persuaded Sister to decorate his apartment. After successfully completing this she couldn't really say no to the hotel.

Coleman wanted the hotel to seem more like a grand house, so they discarded the first rule of hotel design – that everything is robust. They did, however, decide to use reproduction furniture rather than antiques, which was probably a very practical decision. In the lobby antique English pine panelling was used with a Brunschwig & Fils fabric on the walls. It could almost have been the hall of a country house. The same feeling pervaded the guest rooms. The Jockey Club was the hotel restaurant and treated slightly differently. It was given a separate entrance; Mr Coleman wanted a room that was neither too formal and stuffy, nor

ABOVE LEFT Enid Haupt's drawing room, designed as a setting for Tiepolo frescoes bought from a Venetian palace. The room mixed Louis XV and Louis XVI furniture, English pier glasses and a Russian chandelier.

BELOW LEFT Mrs Haupt's bedroom, reflected in a looking glass.

OPPOSITE ABOVE Spaso House, the residence of the United States Ambassador to the Soviet Union.

OPPOSITE, BELOW The Great Hall at Spaso House. The skirted table is a typical Sister Parish detail.

too casual and informal, but one where people would feel comfortable dining. They created a room that seemed always to have been there – it had the patina of tradition. It was panelled in pine and fitted out with reproduction Regency sabre dining chairs with leather seats and backs. They adorned the panelling with numerous eighteenth- and nineteenth-century English pictures, many of which were rather primitive in style. It was remarkably successful. Soon after the New York hotel was completed, Parish-Hadley were asked to work their magic in Boston. In the late 1990s the Ritz-Carlton in New York moved a little way down the street and the old building was converted into apartments, and in Boston the old Ritz-Carlton changed hands and is now the Taj Boston. None of Sister's work survives.

Parish-Hadley were also engaged to renovate and decorate Spaso House in Moscow, the residence of the United States Ambassador, during the ambassadorship of Thomas J. Watson, who served from 1979 to 1981. The residence is about a mile from the Kremlin, tucked away in a quiet square. Built for Nikolay Aleksandrovich Vtorov, a wealthy textile manufacturer, this neoclassical mansion was completed in 1914. Its most striking feature is the Great Hall. Some 82 feet long, this magnificent space with its barrel vaults, scagliola columns and fan lights, all topped by a dome, was still dominated by the original chandelier of Russian rock crystal, thought to be the largest outside the Tsar's palaces.

Thomas Watson was an old client and friend, and a neighbour in Maine. The Watsons had bought their rundown old farmhouse in North Haven in 1962 and with Sister's help renovated it superbly. She used lots of local people: ladies in the village made the curtains; Harry Mills in Dark Harbor did the upholstery; and Sister found a man from Camden who did most of the joinery during the winter, living in the house.

Mark Hampton thought that 'the Getty house in San Francisco illustrates the height of the Parish-Hadley style. It is more elaborate, more ornate, than any other expression

The library of the Getty mansion
in Pacific Heights, San Francisco.

of Mrs Parish's taste, and it is appropriate, after all, for the people who live there.'[14] Situated in Pacific Heights in San Francisco, the house was built in that Victorian version of Italianate. There was a narrow entrance hall, with a closed staircase hall off it, leading to the library-study, its neo-Jacobean panelling painted a ravishing peacock blue. The chintz curtains and valances were equally strongly coloured – brilliant reds, greens and blues – but the design appears rather modern. Strong Regency furniture filled the room. The dining room was an essay in restrained and elegant chinoiserie. Antique Chinese wallpaper adorned the walls and a clever fret frieze below the cornice ensured it fit the room. The Chinese theme continued with an elegant Chippendale looking glass, while brackets carried a small collection of porcelain birds. The star of the room was without doubt the eighteenth-century chandelier, probably Russian, the dozen or so candles set amid swirls of crystal. This opened into the large gold and yellow drawing room. Mark Hampton commented that he had never seen more palatial Georgian chairs, and on how the yellow silk curtains were adorned with huge bows.

Another client was Henryk de Kwiatkowski. Born in Poland, in 1924 at the age of fifteen he was captured by the Russians and sent to a Siberian labour camp. Escaping, he managed to reach Iran and then South Africa, where he boarded the *Empress of Canada* bound for England. The ship was torpedoed but he reached England and joined the Royal Air Force, serving until 1947. In 1952 he went to Canada to work for Pratt & Whitney. A few years later he established De Kwiatkowski Aircraft Ltd and Intercontinental Aircraft Ltd. These companies made him a vast fortune, which Sister helped him to spend.

Kwiatkowski first saw Sister's work while he was staying with Connie Mellon: 'I thought she was a nun – a nun who decorated houses.' He knew exactly what type of decoration he wanted. 'When I finally met her, I confessed

The dining room of the Getty mansion with its chinoiserie wallpaper and exquisite and unusual Russian chandelier.

ABOVE The enormous bay window flooded the library of Conyers Farm with light.

OPPOSITE The living room at Conyers Farm.

that I went for chintz, too, and old but well-preserved English furniture that had seen good – but not better – days. I told her I wanted a place that looked like a well-to-do Englishman's house in the South of France. Sister understood exactly and said, 'A la David Niven! I like that too.'[15] The house he wanted Sister to decorate was still on the architect's drawing board. It was to be converted from what had been the garages to Conyers Manor in Greenwich, Connecticut. Alan Wanzenberg of the New York architects Jed Johnson, Alan Wanzenberg & Associates was commissioned to design the conversion and extensions. Sister went to the site with David Kleinberg, her usual assistant, to meet Wanzenberg and see his plans. He led them through the house and at the end Sister said, 'Where is the front door again?' He pointed and was promptly told, 'Well, you realize of course that the whole house is backward.'[16] Wanzenberg's instant reaction was to think she was quite mad. But Sister explained that if the front door was in that position the parking would be adjacent. 'Who wants to go look out from the living room and see cars?' A few days later Wanzenberg telephoned and told her, 'You're absolutely right,' so the house was turned round. Sister always claimed that she did not understand architecture, but she instinctively understood how houses should be laid out, probably because she knew how to live.

From the generous space that had been a six-car garage Wanzenberg was able to carve a living room of some 40 × 20 feet with a 12-foot-high ceiling. The room was given a very simple cornice, and what had once been garage doors were transformed into spacious French doors opening on to the garden on both sides of the room. Perhaps the room lacked architectural merit: in such circumstances simplicity is often the best policy. The room was painted white and cream, with cream linen or cotton curtains hung from brass rods. A large old tavern table effectively split the room in two. Around the black marble fireplace Sister created a seating group using a blue and white cotton diamond weave which she allied to

a rather bold modern chintz, both from Brunschwig & Fils. The same combination, but in a different weight, was used beyond the table where a nineteenth-century English carpet with a black background anchored the scheme. Before one of the French windows stood a gaming table with simple country Chippendale chairs.

On the eastern side of the house Wanzenberg added a huge double-height bay window, which might have been created by Sir Edwin Lutyens. This flooded the library with light, which wall-to-wall Wilton patterned carpet helped to absorb. Plain cream sofas were teamed up with patterned chairs, in this case covered in Lee Jofa's famous chintz 'Althea'; the bright fresh colours of the hollyhocks seemed almost to glow in the huge space.

The bedrooms, which opened off a hall painted a shade of green, were equally distinct and full of character. Despite Sister's well-documented dislike of yellow bedrooms, the principal guest room here was done in blue and yellow. The main fabric was a chintz from the fabric retailers Clarence House (it was actually a Colefax and Fowler fabric), with bright blue hydrangea flowers on a white and yellow striped ground. The fabric was used to dress the four-poster bed and for window curtains, so it was logical to paint the walls a strong yellow. Yet another guest room was decorated in a blue and white toile from Brunschwig. The pattern was rather large scale and helped to disguise the sloping ceilings and general irregularity of the room.

When Sarah Ferguson, then Duchess of York, visited this house she was so impressed that she invited Parish-Hadley to decorate the Yorks' new home in Windsor Great Park. In the end it was not considered politic that a house belonging to a member of the British royal family should be decorated by an American design firm. After several meetings Parish-Hadley were asked to resign the commission and the decoration was eventually carried out by Nina Campbell. However, Parish-Hadley got a great deal of publicity from the commission.

In March 1992 Kwiatkowski bought the 847-acre Calumet Farm estate in Lexington Kentucky. After the success of Conyers Farm Sister had decorated all his houses – an apartment in New York; a house in Palm Beach, Florida, and a house at Lyford Cay in the Bahamas – so it was natural that he would turn to her for help. When she saw the house she told him 'The possibilities of this house are regal – when we get through with it, it will be fit for a king.'[17] By this time her health was failing, and so she did not take as active a role as usual. It fell to David Kleinberg to do the decoration, with some input from Sister. One morning Barbara de Kwiatkowski got a telephone call from Sister, who cheerfully announced, 'Last night I dreamt about a chintz for Calumet.' It was Sister who selected the pale yellow chintz used in the master bedroom. As Barbara recalled 'I think she had it in one of her bedrooms. I think that meant she liked us. She loved the house.'[18] The renovations took well over a year to complete and by the time it was finished Sister was too ill to travel, so she never saw the end result. But her spirit pervades the fabric of the house, for her influence was everywhere, from the muted green colour, which Barbara de Kwiatkowski referred to as 'our green' (it was used in most of their houses – a green over a cream base), to the bleached pine of the trophy room.

Calumet Farm was the last house with which Sister was involved. In so many ways it encapsulates the Parish-Hadley style, a style that was and remains hugely influential in the United States.

ABOVE LEFT At Calumet Farm a large bay window with whimsical pendant pelmet framed a delightful dining area overlooking the garden.

BELOW LEFT The library, panelled in knotty pine.

RIGHT The trophy room, used as an everyday sitting room. Like the rest of the house, it was largely the work of David Kleinberg, working under Sister's direction.

TWILIGHT

Sister in the 1980s with one of her Pekinese, Rickie.

PREVIOUS PAGES Parish-Hadley 'Dolly' in Parma.

TWILIGHT

Harry Parish had retired to the clearer, purer air of Maine in the early 1970s. After that Sister divided her time between New York and Dark Harbor, spending ten days in Maine and a week in New York. Harry died in 1977. Four years later her son, Henry, died suddenly of a heart attack. He was just fifty. This was a terrible blow for Sister. As her granddaughter observed, 'She never completely recovered. She threw herself into her work, but there was a lasting melancholy over the loss of "little Harry".[1] The loss of her beloved husband and son aged Sister enormously, and she looked increasingly to her daughters, Apple and D.B., for support, becoming less the domineering mother and more of a friend.

Sister was a tireless worker and was constantly busy with one project or another. But ill health and old age gradually caught up with her and in the early 1990s she went to the office less and less. During the winter of 1992–3 she was taken ill and there followed a period in hospital in New York. She was always a dreadful patient, provoking one exasperated doctor to tell her so, only to receive the spirited rejoinder 'And you are the worst doctor that I have ever had!' One feels a certain sympathy for hospital staff, as 'she would sulk, sneer, and take swipes at whatever hospital worker crossed her path.' She would never speak to anyone unless her family were around to engage in secretarial duties, although on one occasion when she was in Pen Bay Hospital in Rockland, Maine, the telephone rang and a slightly flustered member of staff had to remonstrate with her: 'But you have to take it, Mrs Parish. It's an Archbishop Buatta and he says he must speak to you.' She smiled and spoke to Mario Buatta, one of the few decorators she genuinely respected.

In the spring of 1994, after a lengthy period in hospital, she went back to her apartment to be looked after by Apple and D.B., with help from nurses. She gradually deteriorated, losing interest in life, and was often confused, thinking that people who were dead were somehow still alive. In the end her daughters became convinced that if they could only take her to Maine she would recover and be her old self. It was a forlorn hope. As spring gave way to summer Sister longed to go to Maine as she always had, and she seemed to gain some strength, which enabled her to be moved in an air ambulance. The smell of the pine forests and of the ocean were a great comfort to her, but failed to revive her as her family had hoped.

Autumn comes early in Maine, and as the season began to change Sister's life gradually drew towards a close. She died on 8 September 1994. Her funeral was held a week later at the small church she had attended every summer. She was laid to rest beside her beloved Harry, by an old stone wall covered in lichen. Her daughter Apple gave the eulogy in which she quoted an islander who had once described her Mother as 'a tough old turkey', a remark Sister loved. As Apple went on to say, when she was a child her parents told her not to be afraid of the thunder; it was merely 'God and his buddies bowling in their private bowling alley'. Apple now tells her grandchildren not to be afraid of the thunder because 'it's only your great-grandmother moving the furniture around. She's just got another new job and will be hurling things around until it looks just right. Then there will be peace and quiet.'[2]

Sister's memorial service was held at St James's Church, Madison Avenue in New York. As the church bell tolled once for every year of her life, it seemed also to toll for the passing of a way of life. This time her niece Maisie Houghton gave the eulogy, remarking, 'Sister always got it right. The houses she created for her adored family were what drew us all to her. The iced tea or the stiff drink, the pots of primroses, the fire burning brightly, the soft throw on the end of the bed.'[3]

The following year Sotheby's in New York sold the contents of Sister's New York apartment. It was the highlight of that season's calendar. It was a wonderfully eclectic collection and she would have been amazed at some of the prices realized. It showed the breadth of her tastes and interests, but it also showed the depth of her historical knowledge of furniture, porcelain and objets d'art. Whatever she said, she had learnt a huge amount from her father and from all the museum-visiting of her childhood.

As Sister herself wrote, 'A decorator's taste, a decorator's eye, the personality that any decorator expresses in his or her work comes from deep within, some of it inherited, some of it experienced, some of it acquired.'[4] Sister had taste in abundance but, like her friend Nancy Lancaster, she also had something even more important: a great talent for living.

Sister with her daughters, D.B. and
Apple, on the porch of the Summer
House in Maine, just setting off for
a party.

NOTES

WHERE IT ALL BEGAN

1 Morristown was discovered by the New York rich towards the end of the nineteenth century. Gustav Kissel built a large house, Wheatsheaf, on Sussex Avenue and, with his brother, owned several plots of land in the immediate area.

2 Dr Francis Parker Kinnicutt (1849–1913). He was a friend of Edith Wharton.

3 Apple Parish Bartlett, and Susan Bartlett Crater, *Sister: The Life of Legendary American Interior Decorator Mrs Henry Parish II* (St Martin's Press, New York, 2000), pages 9 and 10. Gustav Kinnicutt began his Wall Street career at J.P. Morgan & Co. and went on to found his own firm with his uncle Gustav Edward Kissel (1854–1911); this merged in 1932 into Kidder, Peabody & Company with Gustav Kinnicutt becoming a senior partner. Kinnicutt was a descendant of one Roger Kennicott, who emigrated from Devon to Massachusetts in the 1660s.

4 'Mrs Parish Remembers', *House & Garden* (New York), November 1990, page 162.

5 Bartlett and Crater, *Sister*, page 9.

6 Bayard Tuckerman (1855–1923) was the author of a number of books, among them *History of English Prose Fiction* (1882); *Life of General Lafayette* (1889); *Peter Stuyvesant* (1893); *William Jay and the Abolition of Slavery* (1893); *Life of Philip Schuyler, Major General in the American Revolution* (1903); he also edited *the Diary of Philip Hone* (1889).

7 'Mrs Parish Remembers', page 162.

8 Dorothy Draper (1889–1969), born Dorothy Tuckerman, was a first cousin of Sister's mother. Her father, Paul Tuckerman, was the seventh child of Lucius and Elizabeth Tuckerman and the brother of Bayard. She was born in Tuxedo Park, New York State, and in 1912 she married Dr George Draper, who became personal physician to Franklin Roosevelt.

9 'Miss Tuckerman Married', *New York Times*, 19 April 1907.

10 Sister's three brothers were: Francis Parker ('Frankie') Kinnicutt (1908–1961); Gustav Hermann ('Gory') Kinnicutt (1912–1984); and Bayard ('Birdie') Kinnicutt (1918–1934); Birdie died while playing baseball at St Mark's School.

11 'Mrs Parish Remembers', page 160.

12 John K. Turpin and W. Barry Thomson, *New Jersey Country Houses: The Somerset Hills* (Mountain Colony Press, 2005), page 166.

13 Bartlett and Crater, *Sister*, page 25.

14 Bartlett and Crater, *Sister*, pages 25–6, 27.

15 'Mrs Parish Remembers', page 164.

16 The papers of Ellen Shipman (1869–1950) are held at Cornell University. There are no surviving planting plans for Mayfields and only five photographs are listed, all of them copies of photographs taken by John Wallace Gillies and published in *House Beautiful* in February 1923. The papers of Marian Cruger Coffin (1876–1957) are held in the library at Winterthur and they contain three photographs of Mayfields, all duplicates of the Gillies' photographs already mentioned.

17 Sister Parish, Albert Hadley and Christopher Petkanas, *Parish-Hadley: Sixty Years of American Design* (Little Brown, New York, 1995), page 12.

18 Bartlett and Crater, *Sister*, page 41. Sister places her coming-out party in the Pierre Hotel, but this must be a mistake, as the hotel was not opened until 1930.

19 Bartlett and Crater, *Sister*, pages 40–41.

20 Bartlett and Crater, *Sister*, page 43.

21 Bartlett and Crater, *Sister*, page 44.

22 Bartlett and Crater, *Sister*, page 50.

IN TRADE

1 Clarence Dillon (1882–1979) was one of the richest men in America. He was an investment banker, a partner in Dillon, Read & Co, in which he bought a majority interest in 1916. During the First World War he was Assistant Chairman of the War Industries Board. A Francophile, in 1929 he bought an apartment in

Paris and in 1935 he paid 2.3 million francs for Château Haut-Brion, which produced his favourite wine. He bought the Dunwalke estate in Far Hills, New Jersey, in 1920.

2 Syrie Maugham was famous for her white room, created in about 1927–8 at her house in the King's Road, Chelsea. The room was actually not all white but a confection of tints and tones from white to beige. It caused a minor sensation when it appeared in *Harper's Bazaar* in October 1929. By 1936 Syrie had transformed her white room into a red and white room. Sister's sitting room was very much a product of its time and a reflection of fashionable taste.

3 Bartlett and Crater, *Sister*, page 61.

4 Virginia Lee Warren, 'Sister Parish Creates Distinctive Interiors by Instinct', *New York Times*, 18 May 1965, page 42.

5 Turpin and Thomson, *New Jersey Country Houses*, page 328; and *The Connoisseur*, February 1952, page 77. Sister shared the building with a Mrs Frederick W. Jones, who ran a dress shop.

6 Bartlett and Crater, *Sister*, page 66.

7 Bartlett and Crater, *Sister*, page 66; Jane S. Hylicke, New Jersey Librarian, Bridgewater Library, Somerset County, New Jersey.

8 Howard Dearing Johnson bought a small store selling sweets, newspapers and patent medicines in Wollaston, Boston, Massachusetts, in 1925. He developed a range of ice cream with a 'secret' formula (actually, the 'secret' was a butterfat content almost twice the usual standard). He opened his first restaurant in Quincy, Boston, but he lacked the capital to expand further. In 1935 he persuaded a friend to open a restaurant under a franchise agreement in Orleans, on Cape Cod. Within a year there were four 'Howard Johnson's' restaurants. By the close of 1936 thirty-nine franchised restaurants had been opened and in 1939 there were over hundred outlets all along the eastern seaboard.

9 Albert Hadley, interview with the author, 23 March 2010. He believes that Sister set up Budget Decorators with three or four friends from Far Hills, but he has no recollection of – probably never knew – who the other members of the partnership were.

10 Bartlett and Crater, *Sister*, pages 72–3.

11 Mark Hampton, *Legendary Decorators of the Twentieth Century* (Robert Hale Ltd, London, 1992), page 203.

12 Bartlett and Crater, *Sister*, page 73.

13 *Vogue*, July 1960, page 118.

14 Vincent Astor's parents were John Jacob Astor IV and his first wife, Ava Lowie Willing, a Philadelphia heiress. John Jacob Astor died when the *Titanic* sank in 1912, leaving his son a fortune reputed to be around $200 million. In 1919 his mother married Thomas Lister, Baron Ribblesdale.

15 David Patrick Columbia, 'A Conversation with Mrs Astor', *New York Social Diary*, 1 April 2009.

16 The design Van Day Truex produced was manufactured by Edward Fields, Inc., and was christened 'Terra'. The pattern was in dark earth tones, to hide stains and dirt from the three Great Danes and the Mexican *burro* which had the run of the house. The carpet is still in production today. Adam Lewis, *Van Day Truex: The Man who Defined Twentieth-Century Taste and Style* (Viking Studio, New York, 2001), page 208.

17 T. Page Cross was the son of Elliot Cross, the architect of Mayfields, Sister's family home.

18 Bartlett and Crater, *Sister*, page 268.

19 *Architectural Digest*, March/April 1974, page 59.

20 Bartlett and Crater, *Sister*, page 270.

21 Bartlett and Crater, *Sister*, page 271.

22 The Trustees of Reservations is a non-profit organization dedicated to preserving natural and historical places in the Commonweath of Massachusetts.

IN SEARCH OF STYLE

1 Parish, Hadley and Petkanas, *Parish-Hadley*, page 19.

2 Parish, Hadley and Petkanas, *Parish-Hadley*, page 21.

3 Bartlett and Crater, *Sister*, pages 140–141. The letter was written on Thursday 1 April 1948.

4 In a magazine article in the late 1970s Sister remarked that 'my first influence was Sibyl Colefax' and that she considered her glazed chintzes 'luscious, mouth-watering. I learned the extraordinary art of understated British comfort from her. I spread her gospel and then added a few footnotes.' There may be some exaggeration here – or perhaps journalistic confusion. It is unlikely that Sister would have ever seen any of Sibyl Colefax's work as a decorator before her 1948 trip to England, when she may have visited her last home in Lord North Street.

5 Bartlett and Crater, *Sister*, page 139.

6 The Haseley Court visitors' books record several visits by Sister. For example, she stayed, with Harry and D.B., for the weekend of 9–11 May 1959. In 1961 she was there, again with Harry, on 15 April. The following year she and Harry stayed from 29 March to 2 April (when another of the guests was John Fowler). In 1963 she

was there, with Albert Hadley, for 22–24 March; on this occasion the other guests were Virginia Ford and Tom Parr of Colefax and Fowler.

7 John Fowler and John Cornforth, *English Decoration of the 18th Century* (Barrie & Jenkins, London, 1986), page 261.

8 Albert Hadley, interview with Barrie MacIntyre, date unrecorded.

DECORATING CAMELOT

1 Bartlett and Crater, *Sister*, page 79.

2 Stéphane Boudin (1880–1967) was president of Jansen from 1936 until 1961. It was probably Jayne Wrightsman who introduced him to Jackie. In a letter to Boudin five years before Kennedy was elected, Wrightsman remarked 'who knows – she [Jackie] may some day be First Lady.'

3 Elisabeth C. Draper (1903–1993) founded the New York decorators Taylor & Low in about 1930 with her sister, Tiffany Taylor. She went on to establish her own firm in 1936. She worked for the Eisenhowers in New York and at their home in Gettysburg. She also decorated the American Embassy in Paris for Ambassador Amory Houghton, who served 1957–61.

4 Gladys Tartiere (1883–1993) was born in Chicago. Her first husband was Ernest Byfield, a Chicago hotel magnate; they divorced in 1928 and in 1929 she married the French banker Raymond F. Tartiere.

5 Thomas Fairfax, 6th Lord Fairfax of Cameron (1693–1781) was the only British peer resident in colonial America.

6 Elaine Broadhurst, letter to the author.

7 Bartlett and Crater, *Sister*, page 82.

8 JFK Library, Parish-Hadley Notes, Box 1.

9 J. B. West, *Upstairs at the White House* (W.H. Allen, New York, 1974), page 236. James Bernard West (1912–1983) started work as Under Chief Usher to President Roosevelt in 1941. He was Chief Usher (running a household of around a hundred staff) from 1957 until his retirement in 1969. *Upstairs at the White House* is an invaluable record of his time there.

10 West, *Upstairs at the White House*, page 193.

11 A Bill was laid before Congress on August 1961 and passed into law (Public Law 87–286) in September of that year.

12 Bartlett and Crater, *Sister*, page 88.

13 James Abbott and Elaine M. Rice, *Designing Camelot: The Kennedy White House Restoration* (Van Nostrand Reinhold, New York, 1998), page 26.

14 Bartlett and Crater, *Sister*, page 88; West, *Upstairs at the White House*, page 199.

15 West, *Upstairs at the White House*, page 199.

16 Abbott and Rice, *Designing Camelot*, page 154.

17 *The White House: A Historic Guide* (White House Historical Association, Washington, D.C., 1987), page 84.

18 John Langeloth Loeb (1902–1996), with his father, founded Carl M. Loeb & Co. in 1931. This was the firm that merged with Rhoades & Co. to form Loeb, Rhoades & Co. in 1937. Henry Parish II was an employee and subsequently a partner in Loeb, Rhoades & Co.

19 Abbott and Rice, *Designing Camelot*, page 168.

20 Keith Irvine, quoted in Bartlett and Crater, *Sister*, page 99.

21 Abbott and Rice, *Designing Camelot*, page 207.

22 West, *Upstairs at the White House*, page 200.

23 Abbott and Rice, *Designing Camelot*. The vaulted ceiling is reminiscent of the work of Sir John Soane, for instance in the State Dining Room at 10 Downing Street.

24 West, *Upstairs at the White House*, page 277.

25 Duncan Phyfe (1768–1854) was born Duncan Fife in Loch Fannich, Scotland. At the age of sixteen he emigrated to Albany, New York, where he was apprenticed to a cabinetmaker. He opened his own business in New York in 1794 and he eventually employed over a hundred workers. Phyfe worked in a variety of styles including Empire, Sheraton, Regency and Federal. Some of his furniture can be seen in the Green Room.

26 West, *Upstairs at the White House*, page 243.

27 Abbott and Rice, *Designing Camelot*, pages 95–6.

28 West, *Upstairs at the White House*, page 246.

29 West, *Upstairs at the White House*, page 244.

30 The custom whereby each new president has a special rug made for the Oval Office seems to be of more recent origin.

31 A plaque on the desk records :

H.M.S. RESOLUTE forming part of the expedition sent in search of SIR JOHN FRANKLIN IN 1852, was abandoned in latitude 74 degrees 41 minutes N longitude 101 degrees 22 minutes W on 15th May 1854. She was discovered and extricated in September 1855 in latitude 67 degrees N by Captain Buddington of the United States Whaler GEORGE HENRY. The ship was purchased, fitted out and sent to England as a gift to HER MAJESTY QUEEN VICTORIA by the PRESIDENT AND PEOPLE of the UNITED STATES as a token of goodwill & friendship. This table was made from her timbers when she was broken up, and is presented by the QUEEN OF GREAT BRITAIN to the PRESIDENT OF THE UNITED STATES as a memorial of the courtesy and loving kindness which dictated the offer of the gift of the RESOLUTE.

32 Heymann, C. David, *A Woman Named Jackie* (Heinemann, London, 1989), page 323.

33 Patrick O'Higgins, 'The Mother of Them All', *New York*, 12 February 1979, page 55.

PARISH HADLEY

1 Albert Hadley, interview with Barrie McIntyre, date unrecorded.

2 Albert Hadley never knew Vaucluse for it passed from the family. In 1917 the Federal Government bought the Hadley estate of 6,000 acres to build the Hickory Smokeless Powder Works to manufacture gunpowder. The works were up and running in just six months, but closed following the Armistice in 1918. Eventually the land was bought by the DuPont Company, and it became a chemical works for manufacturing rayon. The powder works also displaced Albert's widowed grandmother Mathilde, who was forced to leave Gretna Green, the house her husband's parents gave them as a wedding present. A classical-style house built of pale pink bricks which had been hand-made by slaves, it had been furnished in the latest style from shops in St Louis or New Orleans.

3 Parish, Hadley and Petkanas, *Parish-Hadley*, page 28.

4 Parish, Hadley and Petkanas, *Parish-Hadley*, page 28.

5 Adam Lewis, *Albert Hadley: The Story of America's Pre-eminent Interior Designer* (Rizzoli, New York 2005), page 42.

6 Lewis, *Albert Hadley*, page 74.

7 David Kleinberg, interview with the author, 24 March 2010.

8 David Kleinberg, interview with the author, 24 March 2010.

9 In her memoirs Sister mentions the project, Court House in Johannesburg, and having 'a long talk with the famous decorator Mr L [Mr Loerincz of Braamfontein], who couldn't have been nicer'. Everything was bought in England and shipped to South Africa, where Keith Irvine arranged it all according to Sister's instructions.

10 Keith Irvine, interview with the author, 26 March 2010.

11 Valentine Lawford, 'Living with Flowers', *Vogue*, 1 April 1963.

12 Parish, Hadley and Petkanas, *Parish-Hadley*, page 2.

13 Parish, Hadley and Petkanas, *Parish-Hadley*, page 39.

14 Lewis, *Albert Hadley*, page 102.

15 Parish, Hadley and Petkanas, *Parish-Hadley*, page 8. Mark Hampton (1940–1998) later became one of America's leading decorators. Sister was fond of him partly because he reminded her of her youngest brother, 'Birdie', who had died as a young boy.

16 Parish, Hadley and Petkanas, *Parish-Hadley*, page 39.

17 Nancy Novogrod, quoted in Parish, Hadley and Petkanas, *Parish-Hadley*, page 4.

18 Eugenia Sheppard, 'The Quilting Bee of Sister Parish', *Women's Wear Daily*, 16 February 1968.

19 Tricia Jameson, interview with author, date unrecorded.

20 Albert Hadley, interview with the author, 23 March 2010.

21 Parish, Hadley and Petkanas, *Parish-Hadley*, page 8.

22 Libby Cameron, interview with Gillian Drummond and the author, March 2010.

AN IDEA OF HOME

1 Elaine Greene, 'The Country Look is Still Out in Front', *New York Times*, 26 May 1988, Section C, page 1.

2 Elizabeth Lawrence, 'Isleboro: A Bit of the Maine Coast', *House & Garden*, July 1907, pages 17–20.

3 Christopher Petkanas, 'Dark Harbor Days', *House Beautiful*, January 1995, page 114.

4 Greene, 'The Country Look is Still Out in Front', page 1.

5 'Decorating with Spirit: Imagination Country Style', *House & Garden*, December 1977, page 111.

6 Petkanas, 'Dark Harbor Days', page 114.

7 'Living in a Garden Indoors and Out', *House & Garden*, March 1971, page 88.

8 Bartlett and Crater, *Sister*, page 309.

9 Bartlett and Crater, *Sister*, page 311.

10 Bartlett and Crater, *Sister*, page 307.

11 'The Easy-Does-It Crafts of a Talented Family', *House & Garden*, May 1973, page 132.

12 'The Charm of Living in an Up-To-Date Log Cabin', *House & Garden*, February 1974, page 38.

13 'The Charm of Living in an Up-To-Date Log Cabin', page 39.

A PLACE IN TOWN

1 'Mrs Parish Remembers', page 166.

2 Christopher Gray, 'Streetscapes, 39 East 79th Street: A Co-op Built By and For the Social Register Crowd', *New York Times*, 14 November 1999. Emily Post dreamed up the idea of a socially exclusive co-op in 1924. The block was the fulfilment of her ideas.

3 Hampton, *Legendary Decorators of the Twentieth Century*, page 202.

4 'The Great Divide: The Taste for the Cherishable', *House Beautiful*, October 1968, page 116.

5 Hampton, *Legendary Decorators of the Twentieth Century*, page 198.

6 Bartlett and Crater, *Sister*, page 182.

7 Bartlett and Crater, *Sister*, page 183.

8 Bartlett and Crater, *Sister*, page 183.

9 David Kleinberg, 'Sister, Be Praised', *House & Garden*, July 1995, page 68.

DESIGNS FOR LIVING

1 O'Higgins, 'The Mother of Them All', page 56.

2 Bartlett and Crater, *Sister*, page 135.

3 Bartlett and Crater, *Sister*, page 209.

4 The house featured in *House Beautiful* in May 1934. The article includes a floor plan. It also states that Beatrix Farrand designed the gardens.

5 Arthur Schlesinger, Jr, 'Profiles: Brooke Astor', *Architectural Digest*, May 1986, page 167.

6 Parish, Hadley and Petkanas, *Parish-Hadley*, page 39.

7 Susan Bartlett Crater, Libby Cameron and Mita Corsini Bland, *Sister Parish Design: On Decorating* (St Martin's Press, New York, 2009), page 3.

8 Bartlett and Crater, *Sister*, page 226.

9 Bartlett and Crater, *Sister*, page 228.

10 O'Higgins, 'The Mother of Them All', page 56.

11 Christopher Hemphill, 'A Scent of Sun and Flowers', *House & Garden*, September 1985, page 129.

12 Hemphill, 'A Scent of Sun and Flowers', page 129.

13 The executive offices were illustrated in *Interior Design* in April 1971.

14 Hampton, *Legendary Decorators of the Twentieth Century*, page 211.

15 Steven M. L. Aronson, 'Back Country Greenwich', *House & Garden*, August 1987, page 135.

16 Bartlett and Crater, *Sister*, page 138.

17 Steven M. L. Aronson, 'Kentucky Pride at Calumet Farm', *Architectural Digest*, March 1995, page 138.

18 *Courier-Journal*, 4 May 1995, page D1.

TWILIGHT

1 Bartlett and Crater, *Sister*, page 286.

2 Bartlett and Crater, *Sister*, page 337.

3 Bartlett and Crater, *Sister*, page 339.

4 Bartlett and Crater, *Sister*, pages 10–11.

BIBLIOGRAPHY

BOOKS

Abbott, James, and Elaine M. Rice, *Designing Camelot: The Kennedy White House Restoration* (Van Nostrand Reinhold, New York, 1998)

Bartlett, Apple Parish, Susan Bartlett Crater and Mita Corsini Bland, *Sister: The Life of Legendary American Interior Decorator Mrs Henry Parish II* (St Martin's Press, New York, 2000)

Bartlett, Susan, and Libby Cameron, *Sister Parish Design: On Decoration* (St Martin's Press, New York, 2009)

Corbin, Patricia, and Ted Hardin, *Summer Cottages and Castles: Scenes from the Good Life* (E. P. Dutton, Inc., New York, 1983)

Fowler, John, and John Cornforth, *English Decoration of the 18th Century* (Barrie & Jenkins, London, 1986)

Hampton, Mark, *Mark Hampton on Decorating* (Condé Nast, New York, 1989)
    Legendary Decorators of the Twentieth Century (Robert Hale Ltd, London, 1992)

Heymann, C. David, *A Woman Named Jackie* (Heinemann, London, 1989)

House & Garden's Best in Decoration (Random House, New York, 1987)

Irvine, Keith and Chippy, *Keith Irvine: A Life in Decoration* (The Monacelli Press, New York, 2005)

Lewis, Adam, *Van Day Truex, The Man who Defined Twentieth-Century Taste and Style* (Viking Studio, New York, 2001)

Albert Hadley: The Story of America's Pre-eminent Interior Designer (Rizzoli, New York 2005)

Parish, Sister, Albert Hadley and Christopher Petkanas, *Parish-Hadley: Sixty Years of American Design* (Little Brown, New York, 1995)

Pool, Mary Jane, *20th Century Decorating Architecture and Gardens: 80 Years of Ideas and Pleasure from Home and Garden* (Holt, Rinehart & Winston, New York, 1978)

Skurka, Norma, *The New York Times Book of Interior Design and Decoration* (Quadrangle and New York Times, New York, 1976)

Smith, C. Ray, and Alan Tate, *Interior Design in the Twentieth Century* (Harper Collins, New York, 1986)

Smith, Sally Bedell, *In all his Glory: William Paley* (Simon & Schuster, New York, 1990)

Tweed, Katharine (Editor), *The Finest Rooms By America's Great Decorators* (Bramhall House, The Viking Press, New York, 1963)

Turpin, John K., and W. Barry Thomson, *New Jersey Country Houses: The Somerset Hills*, (Mountain Colony Press, 2005)

West, J. B., *Upstairs at the White House* (W.H. Allen, New York, 1974)

The White House: A Historic Guide (White House Historical Association, Washington, D.C., 1987)

MAGAZINE ARTICLES

'A Large House That Looks Small', *House Beautiful*, February 1923

Alsop, Susan Mary, 'Spaso House in Moscow', *Architectural Digest*, January 1988
'Katherine Graham's Capital Life', *Architectural Digest*, December 1994

Aronson, Steven M. L., 'Back Country Greenwich', *House & Garden*, August 1987
'Kentucky Pride at Calumet Farm', *Architectural Digest*, March 1995
'Sister Parish: The Doyenne's Unerring Eye for Warmth and Grace', *Architectural Digest*, January 2000

Blandford, Linda, 'Places in the Heart', *Vogue*, August 1987

Carlsen, Peter, 'A Sense of Rightness', *Architectural Digest*, January 1983
'The Ritz-Carlton Hotel', *Architectural Digest*, September 1983

'The Charm of Living in an Up-to-Date Log Cabin', *House & Garden*, February 1974

Chatfield-Taylor, Joan, 'Sister Parish on Taste: You Can't Acquire it', *San Francisco Chronicle*, 21 October 1981, page 46

Cheshire, Maxine, 'Sister Parish Believes in a Patchwork Poverty Idea', *Washington Post*, 4 February 1968, Section G

'Choice Foil to City Lights', *House Beautiful*, October 1975

Clark, Edward, and Nina Leen, 'The First Lady brings History and Beauty to the White House', *Life*, 1 September 1961

Collins, Amy Fine, 'Decorating Great Dames', *Vanity Fair*, December 1994

'Colors to live with: Soft Twentieth-Century Pastels', *House & Garden*, September 1972

Columbia, David Patrick, 'A Conversation with Mrs Astor', *New York Social Diary*, 1 April 2009

'Comfort is a Whole Way of Life', *House & Garden*, January 1967

'Decorating with Spirit: Imagination Country Style', *House & Garden*, December 1977

'The Easy-Does-It Crafts of a Talented Family', *House & Garden*, May 1973

Eaton, Yvonne, 'To The Manor Born', *The Courier-Journal*, 4 May 1995

Eberstadt, Frederick, 'The Education of Brooke Astor', *Quest*, February 1991

Farnsworth, Marjorie, 'Comfort Amid Grandeur in this Precious Setting', *New York Journal*, 18 July 1959

Filler, Martin, and Christopher Petkanas, 'The Decorators Who Defined Good Taste in Our Time', *House Beautiful*, January 1995

Fleming, John, 'A Passion for History', *House & Garden*, March 1987

'The Great Divide: The Taste for the Cherishable', *House Beautiful*, October 1968

Freeman, Gladys, 'Ferncliff', *Town and Country*, date unknown

Grossman, Loyd, 'Designs on the Duchess', *Observer Magazine*, 13 March 1988

Greene, Elaine, 'Still Out in Front: The Country Look', *New York Times*, 26 May 1988
'The Courage to be Cozy', *House Beautiful*, May 1990

Groer, Annie, 'A Fixer-Upper to End Them All', *The New York Times*, 5 November 2008

'Guest Speaker: Brooke Astor on the Pleasures of Collecting', *Architectural Digest*, March 1982

Hemphill, Christopher, 'A Scent of Sun and Flowers', *House & Garden*, September 1985
'With Propriety', *Architectural Digest*, May 1981

Hewitt, Mark, 'Living with Antiques', *Antiques*, July 1988

Hitchens, Christopher, 'Our House', *House & Garden*, March 1988

'The Home: Room for Every Taste', *Time*, 9 February 1968

Howell, Georgina, 'American Greats', *House & Garden*, September 1988

'Imaginative Elegance on Long Island', *Vogue*, July 1960

Kleinberg, David, 'Sister, Be Praised', *House & Garden* (London), July 1995

Lane, Jane F., 'Making the Rich Look Right', *W*, 14–21 June 1985

Lawford, Valentine, 'Living with Flowers', *Vogue*, 1 April 1963
'The Unsinkable Sister Parish', *House & Garden*, October 1976
'Historic Houses: The Locusts', *Architectural Digest*, March 1979

Lawrence, Elizabeth, 'Isleboro: A Bit of the Maine Coast', *House & Garden*, July 1907

Linden, Patricia, 'Her Eminence', *Town & Country*, September 1988

'Living in a Garden Indoors and Out', *House & Garden*, March 1971

Lodico, Jim, 'Georgetown Landmark for Sale', *Georgetowner*, August 2008

McMillan, Julie Jackson, 'Parish-Hadley', *Design Times*, Spring 1994 (vol. 6, no.1)

Meenan, Monica, 'Decorating is Change', *Town & Country*, February 1971

'Mrs Parish Remembers', *House & Garden*, November 1990

Nemy, Enid, 'Peel Clan: A Nice Thing to Belong To', *New York Times*, 13 August 1979

'New Tradition North of Boston: Detail on a Grand Scale', *Architectural Digest*, March/April 1974

Norwich, William, 'Inside Fergie's Dream House', *Redbook*, February 1989

O'Higgins, Patrick, 'The Mother of Them All', *New York*, 12 February 1979, page 56

Petkanas, Christopher, 'Dearest Sister… Love, Jackie', *Chicago Tribune*, 7 January 1996

Pryce-Jones, Alan, 'The Triumph of Tradition', *House & Garden*, October 1985
    'Sister's New Rooms', *House & Garden*, October 1986

Reif, Rita, 'The Peel Home: Living Graciously With History', *New York Times*, 13 August 1968

Richardson, John, 'A Very Private Collection', *House & Garden*, October 1989
    'Saratoga Purebred', *House & Garden*, July 1991

Schlesinger, Arthur, Jr, 'Profiles: Brooke Astor', *Architectural Digest*, May 1986

Sheppard, Eugenia, 'The Quilting Bee of Sister Parish', *Women's Wear Daily*, 16 February 1968

Siddeley, John, 'Sister Parish talks to John Siddeley', *Connoisseur*, February 1982

'Sister Parish, Reigning Arbiter of Lovely (and Expensive) Things', *New York Times*, Section C1, 11 April 1991

Stephens, Suzanne, 'Passing the Torchère', *Avenue*, April 1989

'Two Ways of Life – Both Country', *Vogue*, 1 March 1955

Vogel, Carol, 'Part and Parcel', *New York Times Magazine*, 19 April 1987

Warren, Virginia Lee, 'Sister Parish Creates Distinctive Interiors by Instinct', *New York Times*, 18 May 1965

Wilson, Susannah M., 'Personal Contributions', *Southern Accents*, April 1991

INDEX

ACKNOWLEDGMENTS

AUTHOR'S ACKNOWLEDGMENTS

This book could never have been written without the help and co-operation of many people. I am extremely grateful to the family of the late Sister Parish for their help, co-operation and encouragement while I was writing the book. Sister's daughters, Apple and Dorothy (D.B), and her granddaughter, Susan Bartlett Crater, have been endlessly kind and patient. I am also very grateful to other members of Sister's family, particularly Maisie Houghton and Michael Kinnicutt. I also especially wish to thank Albert Hadley for all the time and trouble he took on my account. Many thanks, too, to the remaining staff of Parish-Hadley, Carole Cavaluzzo and Nancy Porter.

Grateful thanks are owed to my friend Gillian Drummond for her kind hospitality on my many visits to the United States and for chauffeuring me hither and thither. I am very grateful to Tim Ardern for his hospitality and to Helen and Robert Austin, who have again generously sponsored some of the travel necessary to research the book. And to Wayne English for his generous hospitality on the island of Patmos, where I habitually revise my manuscripts while gazing out (gazing rather too often) over the beautiful Aegean Sea.

I would like to thank Bethany Romanowski, Elizabeth Broman and all the staff of the Cooper-Hewitt National Design Museum Library, Smithsonian Institution. I am particularly grateful to Greg Herringshaw, the Collections Manager, for all his work finding illustrations I wanted – and some things I didn't even know I wanted, but I did!

Thanks also to the following people and institutions: Bradford Central Library; the British Library; Elaine Broadhead, Glen Ora; Libby Cameron; Colefax and Fowler; the Carl A. Kroch Library, Cornell University; Eric R. Fishman, Essex County Country Club; the late Stanley Falconer; Margaret Furniss; Steve Godwin; Kathy Hammer, Astor Courts; Rusty Harper, David Kleinberg Design Associates; the Reverend Brenda Husson, St James's Church, New York; Chippy and Keith Irvine; Tricia Jameson; the JFK Presidential Library; David Kleinberg; Rich Kummerlowe; Barrie MacIntyre; Manchester Metropolitan University Library; Father Philip Millar; New York Public Library; Jane Hylicke, New Jersey Librarian, Somerset County Library System; Northeast Harbor Library, Maine; Derek Ostergard; Hugo Pineda; Rod Pleasants; Margaret Taliaferro; Judith Tankard; David Taylor, the Ritz-Carlton Hotel, New York; Imogen Taylor; W. Barry Thomson; the National Art Library at the Victoria and Albert Museum, London.

And finally thanks to the unseen hands at Frances Lincoln Ltd who make books possible: John Nicoll and Andrew Dunn; my editor, Jo Christian; the wonderful Sue Gladstone, who is such a wizard with the picture research; and the designers, Becky Clarke and Caroline Clark, who create such a beautiful finished product. And also to my agent, Catriona Wilson, who stops me going bankrupt.

PHOTOGRAPHIC ACKNOWLEDGMENTS

With the exception of those listed on this page, all the photographs in this book are copyright © The Estate of Mrs Henry Parish II. The Publishers have made every effort to contact holders of copyright works. Any copyright holders we have been unable to reach are invited to contact the Publishers so that a full acknowledgment may be given in subsequent editions. For permission to reproduce the images below, the Publishers would like to thank the following.

Photo Eric Bowman © Cooper-Hewitt, National Design Museum, Smithsonian Institution/Art Resource, NY/Scala, Florence: 186 above, 186 below, 187

Colefax and Fowler Archive: 52, 53

© 2011 Cooper-Hewitt, National Design Museum, Smithsonian Institution/Art Resource, NY/ Scala, Florence: 38 left, 38 right, 39 below, 154

Photo Billy Cunningham (www.billycunninghamphotography.com): 152, 156 left, 156–7, 158, 159, 160–61, 162, 163 above, 163 below

Photo Oberto Gili, © 2011 Cooper-Hewitt, National Design Museum, Smithsonian Institution/Art Resource, NY/Scala, Florence: 145, 169 below, 171 above, 171 below

Photo Todd Gipstein/National Geographic/Getty Images: inset to front jacket and 172

Photo Grigsby © 2011 Cooper-Hewitt, National Design Museum, Smithsonian Institution/Art Resource, NY/Scala, Florence: 114 left, 114 right, 119

Photo K. Haavisto © 2011 Cooper-Hewitt, National Design Museum, Smithsonian Institution/ Art Resource, NY/Scala, Florence: 185

Photo John M. Hall © 2011 Cooper-Hewitt, National Design Museum, Smithsonian Institution/Art Resource, NY/Scala, Florence: 174

Photo Horst © 2011 Cooper-Hewitt, National Design Museum, Smithsonian Institution/Art Resource, NY/Scala, Florence: 113, 118 right, 122, 129

Robert Knudsen, White House/John F. Kennedy Presidential Library and Museum, Boston: 69 below, 72, 76 below, 77 above, 77 below, 79, 80 left, 80–81, 83 below, 84, 85

Photo Amy Meadow and Pierre-Gilles Vidoli © 2011 Cooper-Hewitt, National Design Mueum, Smithsonian Institution/Art Resource, NY/Scala, Florence: 182, 183

Maisie Houghton: 14, 16 below

Derry Moore: 58–9 (courtesy *Architectural Digest*), 172

Private collection: 46, 48, 49 left, 49 above right, 49 below, 51, 54, 55, 56, 57, 58, 60, 61

Photo K. Radkai © 2011 Cooper-Hewitt, National Design Museum, Smithsonian Institution/ Art Resource, NY/Scala, Florence: 178, 179 above, 179 below, 180 above, 180 below, 184

Courtesy Sotheby's: 146, 147, 148 above left, 148 below, 149

Photo William P. Steele © 2011 Cooper-Hewitt, National Design Museum, Smithsonian Institution/Art Resource, NY/Scala, Florence: 164 above, 164 below, 165, 166, 167, 175, 176, 177

Cecil Stoughton, White House/John F. Kennedy Presidential Library and Museum, Boston: 64, 73

© Elizabeth Winn: 50